PENGUIN BOOKS

FRENCH COUNTRY COOKING

Elizabeth David discovered her taste for good food and wine when she lived with a French family while studying history and literature at the Sorbonne. A few years after her return to England she made up her mind to learn to cook so that she could reproduce for herself and her friends some of the food that she had come to appreciate in France. Subsequently, Mrs David lived and kept house in France, Italy, Greece, Egypt and India, as well as in England. She found not only the practical side but also the literature of cookery of absorbing interest and studied it throughout her life.

Her first book, *Mediterranean Food*, appeared in 1950. *French Country Cooking* followed in 1951, *Italian Food*, after a year of research in Italy, in 1954, *Summer Cooking* in 1955 and *French Provincial Cooking* in 1960. These books and a stream of often provocative articles in magazines and newspapers changed the outlook of English cooks for ever.

In her later works she explored the traditions of English cooking (*Spices, Salt and Aromatics in the English Kitchen*, 1970) and with *English Bread and Yeast Cookery* (1977) became the champion of a long overdue movement for good bread. *An Omelette and a Glass of Wine* (1984) is a selection of articles first written for the *Spectator, Vogue, Nova* and a range of other journals. The posthumously published *Harvest of the Cold Months* (1994) is a fascinating historical account of aspects of food preservation, the world-wide ice trade and the early days of refrigeration. *South Wind Through the Kitchen*, an anthology of recipes and articles from Mrs David's nine books, selected by her family and friends, and by the chefs and writers she inspired, was published in 1997, and acts as a reminder of what made Elizabeth David one of the most influential and loved of English food writers. A final anthology of unpublished recipes, uncollected articles and essays entitled *Is There a Nutmeg in the House?* was published in 2000. This was followed in 2003 by *Elizabeth David's Christmas*. In 2010, to mark 50 years since publication of *Mediterranean Food*, Penguin published *At Elizabeth David's Table*, a collection of her best recipes and articles, illustrated for the first time with photographs.

In 1973 her contribution to gastronomy was recognized with the award of the first André Simon Memorial Fund Book Award. An OBE followed in 1976, and in 1977 she was made a chevalier de l'ordre du Mérite Agricole. In the same year *English Bread and Yeast Cookery* won Elizabeth David the Glenfiddich Writer of the Year Award. The universities of Essex and Bristol conferred honorary doctorates on her in 1979 and 1988 respectively. In 1982 she was elected a Fellow of the Royal Society of Literature and in 1986 was awarded a CBE. Elizabeth David died in 1992.

FRENCH COUNTRY COOKING
by
Elizabeth David

decorated by
John Minton

Penguin Books

To My Mother

PENGUIN BOOKS

Published by the Penguin Group
Penguin Books Ltd, 80 Strand, London WC2R 0RL, England
Penguin Group (USA) Inc., 375 Hudson Street, New York, New York 10014, USA
Penguin Group (Canada), 90 Eglinton Avenue East, Suite 700, Toronto, Ontario,
Canada M4P 2Y3 (a division of Pearson Penguin Canada Inc.)
Penguin Ireland, 25 St Stephen's Green, Dublin 2, Ireland (a division of Penguin Books Ltd)
Penguin Group (Australia), 250 Camberwell Road,
Camberwell, Victoria 3124, Australia (a division of Pearson Australia Group Pty Ltd)
Penguin Books India Pvt Ltd, 11 Community Centre,
Panchsheel Park, New Delhi – 110 017, India
Penguin Group (NZ), 67 Apollo Drive, Rosedale, Auckland 0632, New Zealand
(a division of Pearson New Zealand Ltd)
Penguin Books (South Africa) (Pty) Ltd, 24 Sturdee Avenue,
Rosebank, Johannesburg 2196, South Africa

Penguin Books Ltd, Registered Offices: 80 Strand, London WC2R 0RL, England

www.penguin.com

First published by John Lehmann 1951
Revised edition 1958
Published in Penguin Books 1959
Second revised edition 1966
Reprinted with further revisions 2001
Reissued in this edition 2011

7

ISBN: 978-0-140-29977-9

Printed in Great Britain by Clays Ltd, St Ives plc

www.greenpenguin.co.uk

MIX
Paper from
responsible sources
FSC
www.fsc.org   FSC™ C018179

Penguin Books is committed to a sustainable
future for our business, our readers and our
planet. This book is made from paper certified
by the Forest Stewardship Council.

CONTENTS

PREFACE TO SECOND EDITION (REVISED)

THIS book was written and published at a time when food rationing was still in full force, and of necessity contained suggestions as to what ingredients might be substituted for quantities of bacon, cream, eggs, meat stock and so on. A list of stores to keep handy and where to buy them was also included, and a few recipes for dealing with tinned foods.

Such advice no longer seems necessary, so these chapters have been eliminated, as well as a few of the longer and more elaborate recipes.

I am anxious to stress the fact that this little collection gives no more than an indication of the immense diversity and range of French regional cookery. It is a subject of such scope that half a dozen large volumes of recipes would scarcely exhaust it. Indeed, it would be almost impossible ever to compile a complete collection, because in France regional cookery is very much alive, and therefore perpetually evolving. As modern transport, changing agricultural methods, and new types of kitchen stoves and utensils make old recipes out of date, so resourceful housewives and enterprising chefs invent new dishes to meet the altered circumstances and to satisfy their own creative instincts where cookery is concerned. But many of these new dishes will be based on the old traditional ones; the ingredients used will be those native to the district; the local flavour will be preserved. And so it comes about that for the collector every visit to France will produce some new dish, and those interested enough will find there is always something new to learn about the engrossing subject of French cookery.

E. D.

INTRODUCTION

A CERTAIN amount of nonsense is talked about the richness of the food to be found in all French homes. It is true that the standard is much higher than that of most English households, but it will not, I hope, be taken as an ungracious criticism to say that the chances are that a food-conscious foreigner staying for any length of time with a French middle-class family would find the proportion of rather tough *entrecôtes*, rolled and stuffed roast veal, and *sautéd* chicken exasperatingly high. For parties and festivals there would be more elaborately cooked fish and poultry, separate vegetable courses and wonderful open fruit tarts; but he would not find many dishes were cooked in cream, wine and garlic – it is bad for the *foie*, he would very likely be told. Those who care to look for it, however, will find the justification of France's culinary reputation in the provinces, at the riverside inns, in unknown cafés along the banks of the Burgundy canal, patronized by the men who sail the great petrol and timber barges to and from Marseille, great eaters and drinkers most of them, in the hospitable farmhouses of the Loire and the Dordogne, of Normandy and the Auvergne, in sea-port bistros frequented by fishermen, sailors, ship-chandlers and port officials; and nowadays also in *cafés routiers*, the lorry-drivers' restaurants.

In such places the most interesting food in France is to be found, naturally, because the shopkeepers, the lawyer, the doctor, the curé, the gendarme and even those stony-faced post-office officials are exceedingly addicted to the pleasures of the table; and, being thrifty as well, you may be sure they know where the cheapest and best of everything is to be obtained. The peasant farmers are prosperous, and not for nothing are they known as the thriftiest people in Europe. Every scrap of food produced is made use of in some way or another, in fact in the best way possible, so it is in the heart of the country that one may become acquainted with the infinite variety of *charcuterie*, the sausages, pickled pork and bacon, smoked hams, *terrines*, preserved goose, *pâtés*, *rillettes*, and *andouillettes*, the cheeses and creams, the fruits preserved in potent local liqueurs, the fresh garden vegetables, pulled up before they are faded and grown old, and served shining with farmhouse butter, the *galettes* and pancakes made from country flour, the mushrooms, *cèpes*, *morilles* and *truffes* gathered in the forest, the mountain hares, pigeons, partridges and roebuck, the *matelotes* of pike, carp and eel and the fried trout straight from the river, the sustaining vegetable soups enriched with wine, garlic, bacon and sausages, the thousand and one shell-fish soups and stews, the *fritures du golfe*, the *risottos aux fruits de mer* of France's lovely prodigal coast, from Brittany to Biarritz and from Spain to Monte Carlo.

Although there is not such a profusion of raw materials in England, we still have much greater gastronomic resources than the national cookery would lead one to suppose.

Rationing, the disappearance of servants, and the bad and expensive meals served in restaurants, have led Englishwomen to take a far greater interest in food than was formerly considered polite; and large numbers of people with small farms in the country produce their own home-cured bacon, ham and sausages; personal supervision of the kitchen garden induces a less indifferent attitude to the fate of spring vegetables; those who have churned their own butter, fed their chickens and geese, cherished their fruit trees, skinned and cleaned their own hares, are in no mood to see their efforts wasted. Town dwellers, who take trouble over their marketing, choose their meat and fish carefully and keep a good store cupboard, are equally interested in seeing that their care is repaid in good and interesting meals.

It is for such people that I have collected the recipes in this book, most of which derive from French regional and peasant cookery, which, at its best, is the most delicious in the world; cookery which uses raw materials to the greatest advantage without going to the absurd lengths of the complicated and so-called *Haute Cuisine*, the *pompeuses bagatelles de la cuisine masquée*, considered the height of good taste and refined living during the nineteenth and early twentieth centuries. Nor is the Technicolor cooking which has partially taken its place in any way an improvement.

Good cooking is honest, sincere and simple, and by this I do not mean to imply that you will find in this, or indeed any other book, the secret of turning out first-class food in a few minutes with no trouble. Good food is always a trouble and its preparation should be regarded as a labour of love, and this book is intended for those who actually and positively enjoy the labour involved in entertaining their friends and providing their families with first-class food. Even more than long hours in the kitchen, fine meals require ingenious organization and experience which is a pleasure to acquire. A highly developed shopping sense is important, so is some knowledge of the construction of a menu with a view to the food in season, the manner of cooking, the texture and colour of the dishes to be served in relation to each other.

The proper composition of a meal being a source of continual anxiety to the inexperienced, I have thought it would perhaps be helpful to include a short chapter on the subject; and as there is no French cooking without wine, its use in the kitchen, unfamiliar to many, is explained in a separate chapter.

The respective merits of *Haute Cuisine*, *Cuisine Bourgeoise*, regional and peasant and good plain, Italian and German, Scandinavian, Greek, Arab or Chinese food are less important than the spirit in which cooking is approached; a devoted, a determined, spirit, but not, it is to be hoped, one of martyrdom.

1950   E. D.

ACKNOWLEDGEMENTS

As any cook must be, I am deeply in the debt of countless cookery writers. In the case of this book I have drawn on several French cookery books for regional recipes. Chief among these are *L'Art du bien manger* by Edmond Richardin, Éditions d'Art et de Littérature, Paris, 1913; *Les Plats régionaux de France* edited by Austin de Croze; *La Bonne cuisine du Périgord* by La Mazille, Flammarion, 1929; *La Cuisine du pays; Armagnac, Béarn, Bigorre, Landes. Recettes recueillies par Simin Palay*, published at Pau, 1937; Pampille's *Les Bons plats de France*, A. Fayard, Paris; and Reboul's *La Cuisinière provençale*, Tacussel, Marseille. My grateful thanks are due to Messrs Allen and Unwin and to Madame Janet Biala for permission to reproduce an extract from Ford Madox Ford's *Provence*. The passage from Gertrude Stein's paper on Raoul Dufy, published in *Harper's Bazaar* for December 1949, is quoted with the permission of Carl van Vechten, Miss Stein's literary executor. I also wish to express my gratitude to the editors and publishers of *Harper's Bazaar* and *Contact* for allowing me to reprint recipes which first appeared in those magazines, and to Messrs Saccone and Speed for permission to reproduce here the chapter on 'Wine in the Kitchen', most of which was originally published by them.

E. D.

TABLE OF EQUIVALENT GAS AND ELECTRIC OVEN TEMPERATURES

Gas	Electricity (degrees Fahrenheit)
¼	241
½	266
1	291
2	313
3	336
4	358
5	379
6	403
7	424
8	446
9	469
10	513
11	536
12	550

BATTERIE DE CUISINE

BATTERIE DE CUISINE

Delicious meals can, as everybody knows, be cooked with the sole aid of a blackened frying-pan over a primus stove, a camp fire, a gas-ring or even a methylated spirit lamp. This book, however, is for those whose ambitions lie in the direction of something less primitive in the way of food, so the question of stocking the kitchen with good pans and the right implements is of the first importance.

If you are starting from scratch, the most satisfactory method is to see that you have the basic necessities to begin with and buy gradually as you find out which style of cooking best suits your talents. (If, for example, you have no particular flair for cakes and pastries, it is pointless to clutter up the kitchen with a whole range of pastry boards, cake tins, tartlet moulds and icing sets.)

One thing is quite certain, and that is that if Englishwomen paid more attention to having the right equipment in their kitchens, we should hear a great deal less about the terrible labour of good cooking. How many times have I been told: 'Oh, I haven't time to fiddle about with that kind of thing', just because a recipe called for putting something through a sieve or chopping up a few vegetables. Don't hamper your cooking and waste time and materials through lack of the right tools for the job.

First, and these are essential to any kitchen, come the very best quality of cook's knives. You need a small vegetable knife, razor sharp, a medium one for trimming meat and fish (known as a filleting knife), a large one for cutting up meat and poultry, and a long, thin-bladed ham knife for cold meat, and anything which has to be thinly sliced. A first-class bread knife goes without saying; keep it for bread. Take the greatest care of your knives; don't cut with them on an enamel or marble-topped table or a plate; have a good steel for sharpening; keep your kitchen knives in a special box or compartment of the knife drawer; wash, dry, and put them away, with the points stuck into a cork, as soon as you have finished with them. Let it be understood by all members of the household that there will be serious trouble if your knives are borrowed for screwdriving, prising open packing-cases, cutting fuse wire or any other purpose for which they were not intended.

Your saucepans will, of course, depend upon your personal preference – or prejudice – as well as upon your cooking stove.

Many cooks, professional and amateur, still cling to the tradition that for serious cooking copper pans are unequalled. While it is true that copper is the best of heat conductors and is exceedingly hardwearing, the almost superstitious belief that possession of a set of copper pans of itself constitutes some guarantee of successful cooking has led to the widespread sale in this country of lightweight copper pots which are soon discovered by the aspiring cook to be of little more than ornamental value. On the other hand the recent dramatic rise in world prices of copper has put saucepans of the requisite heavy gauge copper beyond the reach of all but the most luxuriously equipped of kitchens – not invariably the kitchens from which emerges the most inspired of cookery. I would therefore advise those seeking the best value in basic kitchen equipment to confine their initial purchases of copper to one or perhaps two heavy copper sauté pans about 4 inches deep and 10 to 12 inches in diameter, with or without an improvised lid (the professional chefs' sauté pan does not have, and if used only for its specific purpose, does not need, a lid). Such a pan serves many uses, from the rapid sautéing of small cuts of meat to the lengthy cooking of a fish stew or *matelote* or of a *coq au vin*, and stands up well to roughish treatment.

A straightforward saucepan of 1–2 pint capacity, of heavy quality and with a well-balanced handle, is another asset to anyone who intends to practise serious sauce-making. If this pan is to be a copper one, it is important that the tinning be kept in good condition, so for stirring use a wooden spoon or spatula rather than a whisk which scratches and quickly wears out the tin.

The more experienced cook, progressing to specialized work, may want to invest in the traditional untinned hemispherical copper egg bowl which is unequalled for the successful beating of egg whites but not easy to keep in immaculate condition. An untinned heavy quality (and unless it *is* heavy quality, a minimum of one-sixteenth of an inch thick, don't bother with it) preserving pan is another worthwhile buy, and so, for the ambitious pastry cook or confectioner, is an untinned, lipped, sugar-boiling pan. It should be noted that it is because the melting point of tin is lower than the boiling point of sugar that copper pans for jam-making, confectionery and sugar-work generally are never tinned. To clean untinned copper, rub with a cut lemon dipped in fine salt, or with a soft rag dipped in a strong solution of vinegar and salt.

Certain silver-lined copper pans of Swiss origin now to be found on the English market are of very fine quality and design. These elegant casseroles, sauté pans and marmites are hand finished and have a great allure. They are the modern equivalents of, and will last as long as, the beautiful silver or Sheffield-plate kitchen and dining room treasures – the brandy-warmers, the butter melters, the chafing dishes – of the eighteenth and nineteenth centuries. In other words they are collectors pieces at collectors prices.

Silver linings of copper pans tarnish quickly but are easy to clean (use a silver-polishing cloth) and need less frequent renewal than tin linings. Better than either are the heavy stainless steel linings which need no upkeep at all and should last for ever.

Heavy copper, cast aluminium, and cast iron pans with machine-turned bases are all suitable for all types of cooking stoves. So is stainless steel, but it is a bad heat conductor and to be efficient a stainless steel pan must be heavily copper-clad on the base, which makes for enormous and, it seems to me, unnecessary expense.

Whether you choose cast aluminium, enamelled steel, tinned copper, enamelled cast iron or stainless steel, be sure to have at least two deep stew pans, one large and one small, with a small handle at each side; in these all manner of soups and stews can be put in the oven as well as on top of the stove, an essential requirement for anyone who has other duties than those of a cook to attend to. For boiling potatoes keep one special pan with an enamel lining. Another essential is a shallow oval or round fireproof pan which will go under the grill or in a very hot oven for dishes which are to be browned quickly. One large pan of a minimum 1½ gallon capacity is a necessity for cooking rice and spaghetti, and for anything over four people you must have a still larger one, say 2 to 3 gallons' capacity, and this will do for the boiling of chickens and for making stock. Shallow, two-handled pots from seven to ten inches in diameter and about three inches deep for risotto, pot roasts, various forms of ragoûts and vegetable dishes are a blessing. These can be found in copper, cast aluminium or, better still, enamel-lined cast iron with machine-turned bases.

Earthenware casseroles and terrines for oven cooking should be in every household; for some of the French farmhouse and peasant dishes described in this book they are essential; cassoulets, choux farcis, daubes and civets, lose something of their flavour and a good deal of their charm if cooked in an ordinary saucepan. Earthenware pots can be put on the top of gas and electric stoves, provided an asbestos mat or the more solid modern fireclay simmer-plate is put underneath. The important point to remember is never to pour cold water into one of these casseroles while it is hot, or it will crack.

For eggs, good frying and omelette pans are obviously needed, and little dishes for eggs en cocotte. Plain white, fireproof porcelain or glass egg-dishes can be found in various sizes, and these are the most satisfactory for baked eggs and eggs *sur le plat*, as the egg does not stick as it does to earthenware. The larger sizes are useful for an infinite variety of little dishes. Three frying-pans and one omelette pan are not too many, and they should all be heavy, with a perfectly flat bottom, or the food will never be evenly fried. Have one general-purpose ten- to twelve-inch frying-pan, preferably with a lip so that it is easy to pour off the fat; one which is kept for steaks and cutlets and so on; one small one (say six inches) for frying a few croûtons for soup or anything else to be done in small quantities.

Heavy wrought-iron pans with curved inner walls are still used for the cooking of omelettes and for many other routine frying purposes in most households and in every restaurant in France. Professional chefs, however firm their attachment to copper stewpans and saucepans, do not use copper omelette pans except for the table-lamp cooking of *crêpes Suzette*, steak Diane and similar flambé dishes. Iron pans for omelettes or restaurant frying are now imported in some quantity from France. English-made frying-pans of the same type are to be approached with caution. Although cheap they are often unsatisfactory because the manufacturers have failed to grasp the importance of balance where the weight and the angle of the handles are concerned. A frying-pan with an over-heavy handle looks and feels impressive in the hand but topples sideways when put on the stove, and to the household cook is just one more source of unnecessary aggravation.

A certain amount of superstition still hangs about the so-called 'proving' and maintenance of iron pans. There are still those who recommend that a new pan be rubbed with coarse salt (a first-class way of ensuring instant wreckage of a new pan) or be filled with salt and water to be left boiling for an hour or two. Such advice should not be taken seriously. Salt corrodes, pits, and discolours the burnished metal. Perhaps it is not generally understood that when these pans leave the factory they are coated with a protective film of grease which should be left undisturbed until the pan reaches the customer's kitchen. A preliminary cleaning with a rag, detergent, and hot water removes the superficial grease and any remainder is easily dealt with by heating a generous amount of oil or lard in the pan for a few minutes. Leave this to cool, pour it off, rub the pan clean with newspaper or kitchen tissues, and dry it thoroughly. Once cleaned of its grease the pan is used like any other pan, but when not in use should be kept greased or oiled so that the risk of rust is eliminated. The legend that an iron omelette pan should never be washed owes its origin and perpetuation to this risk and to the high incidence of scratching and scoring induced by drastic scouring, incomplete drying, consequent rust spots, and eventual ruination of the smooth surface of the pan.

Because a correctly made omelette comes away clean from the pan, a pan used and kept exclusively for omelettes by a deft cook does not require washing. Should the necessity arise (and it is unrealistic to assume that we are all perfectly accomplished cooks all of the time) it is infinitely preferable to give your pan a mild scrub in soap and water than to scrape away at it with a knife or savage it with coarse wire wool (fine steel wool should do no harm, but a well-worn Scotch-Brite or Scat pad is better) in the mistaken belief that so long as no water touches your pan no harm can come to it. Whatever method of cleaning is adopted, whether it is a quick rinse or a rub with paper, remember to dry the pan thoroughly and unless it is in daily use to brush the inside with a film of oil or fat before it is put away. The same treatment should be applied to iron paëlla pans and pancake pans.

Anyone who feels that there is too much palaver involved in the regular use of an iron frying-pan would perhaps do best to invest in a heavy cast aluminium all-purpose frying-pan and keep an iron pan only for omelettes. Personally, I use cast aluminium, French enamelled cast-iron and plain iron with impartiality and do not reserve one pan exclusively for omelettes.

For a two-egg omelette, use a 6 to 7 inch pan, for three eggs a 9 to 10 inch pan, for five eggs a 12 inch pan. After that, unless you are a professional omelette cook, make two or three omelettes rather than attempt the tricky task of making a gigantic omelette in a 14 to 15 inch pan which, however well-proportioned, is cumbersome and unwieldy until you become accustomed to the handling of large and heavy pans.

A deep frier with a basket is necessary for chips and for the deep frying of fritters and fish, and for lifting fried food out of the pan you need a perforated ladle or wire skimmer.

When frying is finished, pour off all fat through a small strainer kept specially for this purpose. Keep different kinds of fat separately – a bowl for bacon fat, another for beef dripping, one for mutton and one for pork fat; each has its individual use and should never be mixed.

For poaching a whole large fish, such as salmon or an outsize bass, you need a long narrow fish-kettle with an inner drainer on which the fish rests, so that it can be lifted out of the pan and drained without fear of breakage. Fish kettles are expensive, but are to be found now and again at sales and in junk shops. Oval gratin dishes in varying sizes for baking and grilling fish are easy to find, in earthenware, china or metal, or enamel-lined cast iron. A long platter for serving fish is important; the appearance of a fine salmon, trout or bass is ruined by being brought to table on too small a dish.

The question of kitchen tools is one which must depend on personal preferences, and I cannot do more than enumerate those which through long use and the saving of countless hours I regard with especial affection.

First of these is a purée-maker or food mill. For soups, sauces, fruit and vegetable purées this is absolutely invaluable; in two minutes you have a purée which would take 30 minutes' bashing to get through an ordinary sieve. The best and cheapest of these is a French one, called the *mouli*, and the medium size, about £1.50, is the one for a small household. Even if you have an electric blender you will probably find that you still need, and use, a *mouli*. Then there is a vegetable slicer which goes by the charming name of *mandoline*. If you have ever spent an hour slicing a cucumber paper-thin, or cutting potatoes for *pommes Anna* or *pommes soufflés*, go and buy one of these – a whole cucumber can be done, thinner than you could ever do it with a knife, in a minute or two.

Vegetable choppers are now obtainable in England; called in France a *hachoir*, in Italy a *mezzaluna*, these instruments are crescent-shaped blades with a handle at each end. They make the fine chopping of onions, meat, parsley and vegetables the affair of a second. For small quantities of parsley and other fresh herbs a solid wooden bowl with its own crescent-bladed knife is invaluable. This is called a *hachinette*.

Electric mixers, mincers, vegetable shredders and potato peelers proliferate on the market. For the small household and for beginners the French Moulinex machines offer the best value, the widest choice and the maximum ingenuity. Their recently introduced Moulinette automatic chopper is a particularly valuable machine which performs just what it promises. That is, it chops raw as well as cooked meats without squeezing out their juices or turning them into an emulsion. The new Mouli large-capacity electrical potato peelers are useful if not precisely beautiful.

A good pair of scales, a measuring jug, a first-class pliable stainless steel palette knife, a perforated slice, a pepper mill and a salt mill are obvious necessities; so is a selection of wooden spoons and a pair of kitchen scissors, two or three fine strainers in different sizes, and a clock. A perforated spoon for draining anything which has cooked in deep fat is a great boon; a good solid chopping-board, at least twelve inches by eighteen inches, you must have, and either a wood or marble pestle and mortar.

A rather large selection of cooking and mixing bowls I insist on having – there can't be too many in any kitchen – and the same goes for a collection of air-tight plastic boxes for storing vegetables, salads and fresh herbs in the refrigerator. A supply of muslin squares for draining home-made cheese and for straining aspic jelly, an extra plate rack for saucepan lids, some oven-proof plates and serving dishes, glass store jars in all sizes and a supply of heavy quality greaseproof paper are all adjuncts of a good working kitchen. Aluminium foil we now take for granted, but less well known, and very clean and satisfactory for storage as well as for cooking, are Porosan bags – also ideal, incidentally, as sandwich and picnic food wrappers.

As time goes on you accumulate your own personal gadgets, things which graft themselves on to your life; an ancient thin-pronged fork for the testing of meat, a broken knife for scraping mussels, a battered little copper saucepan in which your sauces have always turned out well, an oyster knife which you can no longer afford to use for its intended purpose but which turns out to be just the thing for breaking off hunks of Parmesan cheese, a pre-war sixpenny tin-opener which has outlived all other and superior forms of tin-opening life, an earthenware bean-pot of such charm that nothing cooked in it could possibly go wrong.

Some sensible person once remarked that you spend the whole of your life either in your bed or your shoes. Having done the best you can by shoes and bed, devote all the time and resources at your disposal to the building up of a fine kitchen. It will be, as it should be, the most comforting and comfortable room in the house.

WINE IN THE KITCHEN

Nobody has ever been able to find out why the English regard a glass of wine added to a soup or stew as a reckless foreign extravagance and at the same time spend pounds on bottled sauces, gravy powders, soup cubes, ketchups and artificial flavourings. If every kitchen contained a bottle each of red wine, white wine, and inexpensive port for cooking, hundreds of store cupboards could be swept clean for ever of the cluttering debris of commercial sauce bottles and all synthetic aids to flavouring.

To the basic sum of red, white and port I would add, if possible, brandy, and half a dozen miniature bottles of assorted liqueurs for flavouring sweet dishes and fruit salads, say Kirsch, Apricot Brandy, Grand Marnier, Orange Curaçao, Cointreau and Framboise. Sherry is a good addition, but should be used in cooking with the utmost discretion; it is vain to think that the addition of a large glass of poor sherry to the contents of a tin of soup is going to disguise it.

THE COOKING OF WINE

The fundamental fact to remember about the use of wine in cooking is that the wine is *cooked*. In the process the alcohol is volatilized and what remains is the wonderful flavour which perfumes the dish and fills the kitchen with an aroma of delicious things to come. In any dish which does not require long cooking the wine should be reduced to about half the quantity originally poured in the pan, by the process of very fast boiling. In certain soups, for instance, when the vegetables have been browned and the herbs and spices added, a glass of wine is poured in, the flame turned up, and the wine allowed to bubble fiercely for two or three minutes; when it starts to look a little syrupy on the bottom of the pan, add the water or stock; this process makes all the difference to the flavour and immediately gives the soup body and colour.

When making gravy for a roast, abolish the cabbage water, gravy browning and cornflour; instead, when you have strained off the fat pour a ½ glass of any wine round the roasting-pan, at the same time scraping up all the juice which has come out of the meat, let it sizzle for a minute or two, add a little water, cook gently another 2 minutes and your gravy is ready.

For a duck, add the juice of an orange and a tablespoon of red-currant jelly; for fish which has been grilled add white wine to the butter in the pan, lemon juice, and chopped parsley or capers; to the butter in which you have fried escalopes of veal add a little red wine or Madeira, let it bubble and then pour in a ½ cup of cream.

TO FLAMBER

To *flamber* is to set light to a small quantity of brandy, liqueur or rum poured over the contents of the pan, which are left to flame until the alcohol has burnt away, leaving a delicately composed sauce in which any excess of fat or butter has been consumed in the flames. The brandy or liqueur will be easier to light if it is first placed in a warmed ladle, to release the spirit, which will then easily catch fire.

TO MARINATE IN WINE

To marinate meat, fish or game is to give it a bath lasting anything between 2 hours and several days in a marinade usually composed of a mixture of wine, herbs, garlic, onions and spices, sometimes with the addition of a little vinegar, olive oil, or water. A tough piece of stewing beef is improved by being left several hours in a marinade of red wine; it can then be braised or stewed in the marinade, strained of the vegetables and herbs which, by this time, have become sodden, and fresh ones added.

A leg of mutton can be given a taste approximating to venison by being marinated for several days. It is then carefully dried and roasted, the strained marinade being reduced and used for the sauce.

For certain *terrines* I always marinate the prepared meat or game for two or three hours in white wine, but red can be used. Hare, I think, needs no marinade, unless it is ancient and tough, as the meat of a good hare has a perfect flavour which is entirely altered by being soaked in wine before cooking, although adding a glass or two of good red wine to French *civet de lièvre*, and of port to English jugged hare, is indispensable.

THE CHOICE OF THE WINE

There is no hard-and-fast rule as to the use of white or red wine, port or brandy for any particular dish. Generally speaking, of course, red wine is better for meat and game dishes, white for fish, but one can usually be substituted for the other, an exception being *Moules Marinière*, for which white wine is a necessity, as red turns the whole dish a rather disagreeable blue colour, and any essentially white dish, such as a delicate concoction of sole, must have white wine.

Incidentally, white wine for cooking should, except for certain dishes such as a cheese fondue, not be too dry, as it may give rather too acid a flavour; and beware of pouring white wine into any sauce containing milk or cream; to avoid curdling, the wine should be put in before the cream and well simmered to reduce the acidity, and the cream stirred in off the fire, and reheated very cautiously.

Don't be discouraged when you read lovely French regional recipes containing a particular and possibly little-known wine; remember that in their country of origin the *vin du pays* is always within arm's reach of the cook, so that while in Bordeaux a *Matelote* of eel is cooked in wine of the Médoc, in Lyons the nuance is altered because Beaujolais is used, and cider in the apple country of Normandy. Here, too, a sweet omelette is *flambéd* with Calvados, in Gascony with Armagnac. In the same way the French frequently employ their own sweet wine, Frontignan, Muscat, or the Vin Cuit of Provence in place of port or marsala.

Cider is excellent for white fish, mussels, for cooking ham, and for rabbit, but it should be either draught or vintage cider.

Cheap wine is better than no wine at all, at any rate for cooking, but the better the wine the better the dish. By this I do not mean that fine old vintages should be poured into the saucepan, but that, for instance, Coq au Vin (see p. 108), cooked in a pint of sound Mâcon or Beaujolais, will be a much finer dish than that cooked in fiery Algerian wine.

If you are going to keep wine especially for cooking, it can be bought in half- or even quarter-bottles.

LIQUEURS

A variety of liqueurs in ounce bottles can be bought by the dozen. A word of warning here – liqueurs in fruit salads should be used with some caution and not mixed too freely, or the fruit will simply be sodden and taste like perfumed cotton-wool.

For soufflés use rather more than you think is needed – the taste evaporates with the cooking. Grand Marnier, Mirabelle and Orange Curaçao are particularly good for soufflés and for omelettes (see p. 157) and, owing to their concentrated strength, can be used when a wine such as Madeira or Sauternes would have to be used in too great quantity for the volume of the eggs.

THE MENU

A list of menus suitable for spring, autumn, summer and winter, for family luncheons, formal dinners, christening tea parties and buffet suppers can never be more than the vaguest of guides; I should be surprised to hear that anybody had ever followed any cookery book menu in every detail; all that is needed to design a perfectly good meal is a little common sense and the fundamental understanding of the composition of a menu. The restrictions of years of rationing have been the cause of some remarkably unattractive developments in the serving of food in restaurants, but if some ignorant or careless restaurant managers still serve chips with spaghetti or boiled potatoes and cauliflowers heaped up in the same dish with curry and rice there is no need for us to do likewise at home; we can plan our dinners round three, or at most four, courses, each one perfect of its kind. In the days of long dinners there were usually two choices at every course, and white and brown succeeded each other monotonously. The idea was right – contrast is important – but contrast in texture and the manner of cooking is more essential than the colour, which was frequently arranged so that roast beef with brown gravy was followed by roast chicken with a white sauce and so on through endless expensively dull food.

Whether or not you are your own cook, it is unwise to have more than one course needing last-minute preparation. When opening the meal with a hot soup, it is perfectly reasonable to follow it with a cold main dish, accompanied perhaps by hot baked potatoes. A dish of hot vegetables, which have been braising in butter in the meantime can succeed the main course, to be followed by a cold sweet. A cold first course can come before a hot dish, which will be simmering in the oven without being spoilt, and can be brought to table with the minimum of fuss. You can then have a cold sweet, and perhaps a savoury, although the savouries acceptable at a dinner party are extremely few, should be very hot and preferably composed of cheese. None of the fishy mixtures spread on tough or sodden toast are in the least welcome at the end of a good meal, in fact the only fish savoury which seems to me worth bothering with is the delicious Angels on Horseback, oysters wrapped up in the thinnest slices of bacon, threaded on skewers, grilled, and served on squares of freshly fried bread, which rules them out for the cook hostess who does not wish to leave her guests while she disappears to the kitchen for ten minutes, emerging breathless and crimson in the face.

Most people can get as far as deciding of what ingredients the meal shall consist, and indeed this is largely dependent on the food in season; the next consideration is the manner of their presentation. A sole cooked in a rich sauce of cream and mushrooms must be followed by a dry dish of entirely different aspect such as a roast partridge or a grilled tournedos, cold ham, jellied beef or a terrine of duck. It must not be preceded by a creamy mushroom soup, nor followed by chicken cooked in a cream sauce. Have some regard for the digestions of others even if your own resembles that of the ostrich. Should you decide to serve your fish grilled, say with little potatoes and an Hollandaise sauce, don't follow it up with another dish requiring potatoes and two more different sauces. The transatlantic manner of serving poultry, game, meat and ham dishes with dozens of different trimmings is simply pointless; the chances are that not one of them will be quite perfectly cooked or sufficiently hot, everybody will have their plates overloaded with half-cold food, and the flavour of the main dish will pass unnoticed amongst the vegetables, relishes, sauces, and salads. One or at most two vegetables are entirely sufficient, and one sauce, nor need potatoes always accompany a meat course. With a roast saddle of hare, for instance, serve a purée of chestnuts, the gravy from the hare, unthickened, but with the addition of a little red wine or port, and perhaps red-currant jelly. Anything else is superfluous. Avoid hot vegetables with anything served in an aspic jelly; if the aspic has been made as it should be with calf's foot and not with artificial gelatine, hot vegetables on the same plate will melt the jelly and make an unattractive watery mess. Potatoes baked in their jackets should be served on separate plates. A delicate green salad, or an orange salad, is the only other accompaniment necessary.

When starting the meal with a hot soufflé avoid serving a mousse at the sweet course; a mousse is only a cold soufflé, and you will have two dishes of exactly the same consistency. In the days of eight courses this was permissible, but with a small meal much more rigid care must be taken.

For the first course, when soup is unsuitable, eggs *en cocotte*, cold poached eggs in aspic, all kinds of *pâté* and terrines, and all the smoked-fish tribe, salmon, trout, eel, cod's roe, and herring are excellent; each accompanied by its particular adjunct, nicely presented hot toast and butter or fresh French bread for the *pâté*, brown bread and butter, lemon and cayenne for the smoked salmon; a creamy horse-radish sauce is the traditional companion of smoked trout, although to my mind this sauce is detrimental to the flavour of the fish.

Any of the sweets made with cream cheese, given on pp. 162–3, make a good ending to a luncheon or dinner, particularly for the summer. Being refreshing and light, they are also appropriately served after such aromatic and satisfying dishes as the stuffed cabbages, on pp. 80–84. Rich chocolate desserts are better served after very light and simple meals.

For the inexperienced cook it seems fairly obvious to say that it is safer when giving a dinner party to stick to something you know you can do successfully, but this doesn't necessarily mean the food need be stereotyped. A little experimenting beforehand will usually show whether a dish is a suitable one to appear at a party; but showing off, however amiably, may well end in disaster. 'Know your limitations' is a copybook maxim which could be applied more often when planning a meal; many a reputation for skilful entertaining has been founded on the ability to cook one dish to perfection; it may be the flair for doing a rice dish, for roasting a duck, or for poaching eggs. The rest of the meal may consist of salad, fruit and cheese, and it will be infinitely preferable to the over-ambitious menu of several dishes, none of which are quite as they should be.

Deep fried food such as soufflé potatoes, cheese *beignets*, and the delicious *scampi* or Dublin Bay prawns in fritters are better kept for days when you have one or two friends who will eat them with you in the kitchen, straight from the smoking fat, the aroma of which is more penetrating than any other cooking smell, permeating the whole house and your own clothes, so it is not for dressing-up days. It should also be borne in mind by the ambitious cook that many dishes served in grandiose restaurants and designed, in fact, for advertisement are not suitable to the small household. Where there is an army of cooks and waiters it may be admissible to make *Crêpes Suzette* at the table and *flamber* them under your dazzled eyes. At home these conjuring tricks are likely to fall flat. Experience, more than anything else, will bring the ability to plan the cooking and serving so that the minimum anxiety and disturbance at the dinner table is compatible with the maximum excellence of the fare.

In this book will be found, I hope, a variety of recipes from which such meals can be composed; soups which can be prepared beforehand and heated up without detriment; a number of simple first-course dishes, always the hardest part of the meal to plan; some noble main dishes in the form of fish, meat, chicken, game and ham cooking, vegetables, eggs, sweets hot and cold, with soufflés for the confident.

A little common sense must be exercised in deciding which dishes can safely be left simmering and which must be served immediately they are ready. It is pointless, for example, to spend time and money on young spring vegetables and then leave them half an hour stewing in the oven; they will have lost all their charm, and it would have been better to serve a purée of dried vegetables. The sterling virtue of punctuality in a cook must give way, if need be, to the greater necessity of keeping guests waiting while last-minute preparations are made.

SOUPS

SOUPS

SOUPE DE LANGOUSTINES D'ORTHEZ

Orthez is in the Béarn, which, with the Pays Basque, made up the ancient Kingdom of Navarre; although Béarnais cooking is much more traditionally French than that of the Pays Basque, their raw materials are similar, and the food has colourful qualities.

Langoustines are the small and delicious shell fish about three inches long, delicate pink, with a very thin shell, resembling Dublin Bay prawns. They are very plentiful in southern and south-western France, and cheap, costing two to three shillings a pound. In England they are not very often seen, and this soup can equally well be made with a small lobster, crayfish, or even prawns.

For four people:

1 lb of any white fish, 1 lb langoustines or lobster, 1 lb tomatoes, 1 glass white wine or cider, 2 lemons, thyme, 2 carrots, 2 onions, 3 or 4 cloves of garlic, paprika or a red pimento, 2 oz rice, 2 eggs, 2 uncooked potatoes, parsley.

Put the white fish and the shells of the langoustines or lobster (keeping the flesh aside), an onion, the carrots, potatoes, herbs, garlic, wine or cider and a lemon cut in slices all together into a large pan, with 4–5 pints of water. Let this simmer for 2 hours at least, so that you have a strong fish stock. Strain it into a clean pan.

Chop up the second onion and the tomatoes and put them into a shallow pan, adding the pimento or the paprika and seasoning, over a low heat without any liquid or frying medium. Cover the pan and cook them until they are reduced to a pulp, which will take about 10 minutes; put this mixture through a sieve into the fish stock. This operation is done separately in order to preserve the flavour of the tomatoes, which if cooked in the stock would disappear. Stir the soup until it is well amalgamated, bring it to the boil and put in the rice. By the time the rice has cooked it will have thickened the soup a little and softened the taste.

Stir in the flesh of the shell fish, cut into small pieces. Have the 2 eggs beaten up in a bowl with the juice of the second lemon; pour a ladle of the hot soup into the eggs, stirring quickly, then add the mixture to the soup, stirring all the time, without letting the soup boil again or the eggs will curdle. At the last moment add a tablespoon of grated lemon peel and a little cut parsley.

This makes a first-class shell-fish soup, reminiscent of the *bisques* of sophisticated restaurants, but not so cloying and, incidentally, a good deal less hard work, as it involves no pounding of shells and sieving of lobster butter; it is smooth and sufficiently thick without needing the addition of cream. With a glass of white Jurançon, or the Vin de Monein, the topaz-coloured wine of the country, or in England with a dry sherry, there is no better way to start off a good dinner.

CRAB OR CRAWFISH SOUP

2 lb tomatoes, 1 lb onions, herbs (if possible sweet basil, thyme and fennel), seasonings (coarse salt, ground black pepper, a pinch of nutmeg and saffron), 1 medium-sized cooked crab, crawfish or lobster, 1 wineglass of white wine, a little cream, 1 oz butter, 2 pints water, a piece of lemon peel, a clove of garlic.

Slice the onions and put them to cook in a little butter; as soon as they are melted put in the chopped tomatoes and all the herbs and seasonings. Cover the pan and leave to simmer for 20 minutes; now add the wine and turn up the flame so that the wine bubbles. After 2 minutes put in half the shell-fish meat, cut in pieces, and add the water. Cook another 15–20 minutes and put all through a sieve. Return the purée obtained to the pan and put in the rest of the shell-fish, finely cut. Reheat the soup, and before serving add the cream or a lump of butter.

SHRIMP SOUP

1 pint cooked shrimps, 2 oz butter, 3 tablespoons white breadcrumbs, 1½ pints fish stock made from the shells of the shrimps, a small piece (about ½ lb) of any white-fish, 1 onion, lemon peel, herbs, salt and pepper, 1 teacup cream or milk, 1 egg yolk, a pinch of nutmeg, the juice of ½ lemon.

Prepare the stock by simmering the fish and the shrimp shells, the onion, herbs and lemon peel in 1½ pints of water for about 20 minutes. Strain it, and put the white breadcrumbs into it.

Pound the shrimps in a mortar with the butter, adding the lemon juice and the nutmeg. Add gradually the stock and the breadcrumbs until the mixture is creamy. Heat it up in a pan for 5 minutes and then press it through a wire sieve.

Beat the egg yolk and the cream or milk together, stir in 2 or 3 tablespoons of the hot soup, return the mixture to the pan and stir until the soup is hot, but don't let it boil.

This is a very delicately flavoured soup and at the same time simple to make. Prawns may be used instead of shrimps.

SOUPE AUX MARRONS

This is the real *Soupe aux Marrons* as it is made in the Pyrenees, and a very different dish from the ordinary purée thinned with milk or stock.

You take a cold roast partridge and pound the meat in a mortar. Roast about 40 chestnuts in a slow oven for a quarter of an hour, shell and peel them and cook them slowly in stock for 2 hours. Then add the pounded partridge meat, amalgamate this mixture by more pounding, and then put it all through a sieve. Return the soup to the pan and let it boil again.

Serve it with fried croûtons.

POTAGE SAINT HUBERT

A fine soup for the days after Christmas, to be followed by the cold turkey or a terrine of game.

1 pheasant, 1 lb brown lentils, 1 onion, 1 leek, 4 oz cream, thyme, bayleaf.

Cook the soaked lentils in salted water with the onion, the white of the leek, the thyme and bayleaf and seasoning.

Roast the pheasant (this may sound wasteful, but an old bird can be used, and at Christmas-time we can surely be a little extravagant), and when it is cooked cut the meat off the bones, and keep aside the best fillets, which you cut into dice.

Pound the meat in a mortar, strain the lentils, add them to the meat; put the mixture through a fine sieve into a saucepan. Moisten it with the lentil stock, adding it until the soup is the right consistency. When it is quite hot add the cream and the diced pheasant.

Any cold game could be used for this soup or the remains of a roast goose. The amounts given will serve eight people.

LA POTÉE

This is the traditional daily food of the peasants of eastern France, particularly in the Haute Marne. It is a simple rustic dish, made from freshly gathered vegetables and home-cured bacon.

It is cooked in a marmite, or heavy iron saucepan; you need a selection of vegetables in about equal proportions, say 12 small potatoes, 12 small carrots, 6 small turnips, and 6 small onions, 2 lb of French beans or broad beans, 2 lb of green peas, the heart of a young cabbage cut in strips, and a piece of home-cured bacon, say about 1 lb for six people.

Put the root vegetables and bacon on first, covered with water, and let them simmer slowly. Thirty minutes before serving add the green vegetables. The cabbage is put in, cut in strips, during the last 5 minutes.

The soup is served in a large deep dish or tureen, the vegetables almost, but not quite, crumbling, and the rose-pink bacon cut into convenient pieces.

SOUPE AU LARD ET AU FROMAGE

Cut ¼ lb of fat bacon in small pieces and melt it gently in a saucepan; when the pieces have yielded enough fat, and before they are overdone, take them out, keep them aside, and into the fat put 6 small onions cut into thin rounds. Cook them very gently until they are almost reduced to a purée; at this moment season the onions and add about 1½ pints of water and leave it to simmer for 30 minutes.

Meanwhile, get ready a number of thin slices of stale bread. Put a layer of these into a deep earthenware casserole or other pan which will go in the oven. Cover the bread with a layer of grated Parmesan cheese, then a tablespoon of fresh cream and some of the bacon; then another layer of bread, cheese, cream and bacon, and so on until the casserole is half full.

Now pour the onions and their stock in the pan and put into the oven for 5 minutes to heat up.

CHOUCROÛTE SOUP

An unusual soup with a pleasant smoky flavour.

1 lb choucroûte *(sauerkraut) or the equivalent of tinned* choucroûte, *2 medium potatoes, 2 rashers bacon, or a bacon bone, or rinds of bacon, pepper, salt, bayleaf, 6 juniper berries, 2 lumps sugar, 1 oz dried mushrooms, ¼ lb uncooked salame sausage or 2 or 3 smoked Frankfurter sausages, 2 pints stock or water, 2 oz cream.*

Put the *choucroûte* into a large pan; add the potatoes, peeled and cut up small, the dried mushrooms, the bacon, or the bacon bone or rind, the herbs and seasonings and the stock or water. Simmer for about 1 hour. Put all through a sieve. Return to the pan.

Cut up the sausage, and cook it in the soup for 15 minutes. Before serving, stir in the cream and, if you like, some grated cheese as well.

MUSHROOM SOUP

½ lb mushrooms, 1 pint water, 1 pint milk, 3 tablespoons flour, 2 oz butter, seasoning, a few bacon rinds.

Make a white sauce with the butter, flour and milk; while this is cooking, bring the water to the boil and put in the washed mushrooms, whole, and the bacon rinds, pepper and salt.

Cook them for about 5 minutes. Strain the mushrooms, keeping the water, and add this gradually to the white sauce. Remove the bacon rinds and chop the mushrooms fairly finely. Add them to the liquid mixture, season, and heat up.

This way of making mushroom soup preserves the full flavour of the mushrooms. It is a mistake to use too many, or to ginger it up with sherry, but a little butter or cream can be added immediately before serving.

ELZEKARIA

A Basque peasant soup.

In pork or goose fat sauté a large sliced onion; add a small white cabbage cut in thin strips, ½ lb of dried haricot beans which have been soaked overnight, 2 crushed cloves of garlic, salt and pepper.

Cover with about 4 pints of water and simmer for at least 3 hours, until the beans are ready. In the Basque country they pour a few drops of vinegar into each plate of soup.

POTATO AND WATERCRESS SOUP

Boil 2 lb of potatoes and 2 onions in 2 pints of water. When they are very soft, pass through a sieve. Reheat, adding ½ pint of milk, plenty of pepper, and a little nutmeg or mace.

Chop 2 bunches of watercress finely and, when ready to serve the soup, add it and stir well in, together with 2 chopped raw tomatoes.

A little white wine, added cautiously so as not to curdle the milk, is a vast improvement.

CHIFFONADE

1 lettuce, chicken or vegetable stock or water, 1 tablespoon rice, 1 oz butter.

Shred the lettuce very small. Melt it in a pan with the butter, and after 10 minutes pour in the stock, and the rice, and cook slowly until the rice is tender. Sorrel can be used instead of the lettuce, or half lettuce and half sorrel.

SOUPE À L'AIL

This is a soup only for those who like their garlic unadulterated. There are a number of ways of cooking *Soupe à l'Ail* throughout Provence and south-western France. This is a version from the Languedoc.

Put 2 tablespoons of goose or other good dripping into a deep earthenware casserole. In this dripping melt gently 24 cloves of garlic without letting them actually get brown.

Pour over them 3–4 pints of warmed stock or water. Season with salt, black pepper, mace and nutmeg. Cook for 15 minutes. Put the soup through a sieve, return it to the pan to heat up. In a bowl beat up the yolks of 3 or 4 eggs with 3 tablespoons of olive

oil. Stir some of the soup into the eggs, then pour the egg mixture back into the soup without letting it boil again.

Have ready prepared some slices of stale bread, toasted in the
oven with the whites of the eggs (not beaten) spread over them.
Put these slices into the soup plates and pour the soup over
them.

MAYORQUINA

Majorca once belonged to the Catalan province which included
the town of Perpignan, where the castle of the Kings of Majorca
is still to be seen. This traditional soup probably dates from
those days. It has all the characteristics of the combined French
and Spanish cooking of this region. It should be made in an
earthenware marmite, which can be left to simmer either on top
of a mat over the stove or in a slow oven.

For five or six people for this soup you need 5 or 6 cloves of
garlic, 2 medium-sized Spanish onions, 1 red pimento, ½ lb
of ripe tomatoes, 2 oz of leeks, the heart of a small cabbage, a
branch of thyme, a bayleaf finely chopped, a clove, 3 tablespoons
of olive oil.

Clean and chop all these ingredients, and peel the tomatoes.
Put the oil into the pan, which should not be so large that the oil
disappears at the bottom, and when it is warmed put in the finely
chopped garlic, then the onions and the leeks. Let this simmer
gently for 10 minutes, stirring with a wooden spoon so that the
vegetables melt but do not brown. Now add the peeled and sliced
tomatoes and the pimento cut into strips, simmer and stir for
another 15 minutes.

Now add slowly about 2½–3 pints of hot water and bring it to
boiling point, at this moment add the chopped cabbage, the
thyme, clove and bayleaf, and salt and pepper, and cover the
pan, leaving it to simmer for 1½–2 hours.

In the soup tureen place several large thin slices of brown or
wholemeal bread. Before serving the soup, stir in a tablespoon
of fresh olive oil and do not allow the soup to boil again. Pour it

over the bread in the tureen, and be sure to have a pepper-mill on the table so that each guest can season his soup to his own taste.

LA FRICASSÉE AND LE FARCI

In the south-west of France, particularly in the Périgord district, the soups are nearly always enriched with a mixture of fried vegetables, onion and garlic, called *La Fricassée*, or *le hâchis*.

A ladle of the vegetables which have cooked in the soup, such as carrots, turnips and onions, are taken out, cut up with a tomato or two, a clove of garlic and some parsley, and perhaps some rounds of raw leek or celery, and sautéd in goose, pork or bacon fat, then returned to the soup before serving, imparting a very special flavour to these *garbures*. When making a soup of dried vegetables, such as lentils or haricots, the *fricassée* will consist simply of a slice of bacon chopped up with garlic and onion, and fried; these simple additions give character and savour to the most ordinary soups.

Le Farci is a stuffing consisting of breadcrumbs which have been soaked in stock or milk, mixed with yolks of eggs, chopped meat, home-cured ham or bacon or salt pork, whatever happens to be available. The mixture is wrapped in cabbage leaves and put into chicken or meat broth to cook for about 20 minutes before serving, giving an added richness and savour to the soup. The *farci* comes out a fine golden yellow from the yolks of the eggs, and is cut into slices, and some put into each plate.

LA GARBURE

This soup, which, like the *Potée*, is rather more of a stew than a soup, is traditional in the Landes, the Béarn, and the Pyrenees. The recipe has many variations, and this one is given as typical of its kind.

In an earthenware casserole, or *toupin* as it is called in the Béarn (a fat comfortable-looking pot, narrowing towards the top, with a straight handle), put ½ lb of bacon, in one piece. Fill the casserole with water, and when it is bubbling throw in the vegetables — say 2 potatoes, 2 leeks, a ½ lb each of shelled peas and broad beans, a turnip, 2 or 3 carrots, all cut into small pieces, a green or red sweet pepper cut in strips, or some paprika pepper, marjoram, thyme, several cloves of garlic. Let all this simmer until the vegetables are half cooked; at this moment add a small white cabbage cut into strips, and a wing or leg of *confit d'oie*, as described on pp. 114–15, or else a piece of *confit de porc* (pp. 97–8), whichever is being used; the fat adhering to the *confit* when it is taken out of the jar is left round it, and imparts its flavour to the *garbure*.

The soup is so thick that the ladle stands up in it; it is served on slices of brown bread in each plate, the solid pieces of bacon and goose being put on to a separate dish and cut up. As each person gets to the end of his soup, he adds a glass of wine to the remaining *bouillon* in the plate, a custom which they call *faire chabrot* in these parts.

Failing either *confit* of goose or pork to add to the *garbure*, make the *farci* as described on p. 29, wrap it up in some of the cabbage leaves retained when the cabbage is sliced, and add these stuffed leaves to the *garbure* at the same time. A few strips of fresh pork rind, tied up in a bunch so that they can be removed, the remains of a roast goose, small garlic sausages, can all go to enrich the *garbure*. In the winter when there are no fresh green vegetables, use ½ lb of white haricot beans which have been soaked overnight.

A few whole roast chestnuts in the *garbure* are a typically Pyrenean addition, and give a most excellent flavour.

The quantities given are sufficient for six to eight people.

L'OUÏLLADE

L'Ouïllade is the Catalan national soup, so called after the *oulle*, the earthenware marmite in which it is cooked, the Catalan version of the Spanish *olla*.

In spite of their somewhat ferocious ways with garlic and strong red peppers, the Catalan country cooking is not without its refinements, as witness this soup, which is, in fact, cooked in two pots at the same time, so separating the flavour of haricot beans and cabbage until the moment of serving.

For four or five people soak 1 lb of white haricot beans; the next day put them to cook with water to cover and let them simmer for about 3 hours. In another pot, with boiling salted water, put a white cabbage cut into strips, 5 or 6 medium-sized potatoes cut in half, 1 or 2 onions, a piece of bacon or a bacon bone, 1 or 2 carrots and a turnip, seasoning and herbs, 1 or 2 cloves of garlic, and a small spoonful of good dripping – bacon or pork fat if possible. The cooking of the second lot of vegetables should be timed so that it is ready at the same time as the beans, which by the time they have cooked should have absorbed nearly all their water. Pour the whole contents of the bean pot into the cabbage and vegetable mixture; remove the bacon bone, stir the soup round, and it is ready to serve.

A little *hâchis* of garlic, onion and parsley, fried in bacon fat, can be added with advantage.

LA SOUPE AUX FÈVES

Take 2–3 lb of broad beans out of their pods, then remove the inner skins from the beans; a fairly long business, but, for those who like the unique flavour of broad beans, well worth it. Bring about 3 pints of water to the boil, salt it, and put in the broad beans. Let the pan simmer slowly. When the beans are half cooked, add a handful of fresh green peas, a few very small white onions and a stick of celery cut in small pieces.

In a separate pan make a little *fricassée* as described on p. 29, with a slice of bacon chopped in small pieces, an onion, a clove of garlic and some good fresh parsley or basil; fry these in bacon fat, and when they are brown add a tablespoon of flour; stir it round two or three times, add a ladleful of the soup, and let it thicken; then return the whole mixture to the soup. Cook it for

10 more minutes. The flour merely gives a little body to the soup, which is not intended to be a thick one.

It is served poured over slices of rye bread in the plates.

CONSOMMÉ FROID ROSE

Put 1 lb of minced lean beef into a pan with 2 lb of tomatoes, 3 pints of meat or chicken stock, seasoning, herbs, and the whites of 2 eggs, let it simmer for 1½ hours and then strain through muslin or cheesecloth, and refrigerate.

There will probably be a little fat on the top, which must be skimmed off. The *consommé* can be made with water instead of stock, and comes out a delicate straw colour, with a really exquisite flavour. The meat and tomatoes can be utilized for a sauce for spaghetti, although the coagulated egg whites make it look rather messy.

ICED SHRIMP SOUP

Make the soup in exactly the way described on p. 23, only omitting the butter and reserving a few of the shrimps whole for the garnish.

When the soup has cooled, add about an inch of peeled cucumber cut into small dice, a little chopped fennel or watercress, and the reserved shrimps. It must be very well iced. Garnish each plate or bowl of soup with a slice of lemon.

FISH

FISH

For all cooking, but particularly for the preparation of fish, vegetables, and for salting meat, *gros sel*, or coarse sea salt, is infinitely
preferable to refined salt. *Gros sel* can be bought by the pound in
Soho shops and in packets at Health Food stores, where one can
also buy the crisp, flaky Maldon salt; this comes in 3-lb packets
and is delicious for the table, necessitating no salt mill. This salt
can also be ordered direct from the Maldon Crystal Salt Co.,
Maldon, Essex.

LOBSTER

During the early summer months, lobsters are in prime condition, and may be bought either alive or dead. As they are very
tenacious of life, and indeed will live on till their substance is
utterly wasted, it is clearly better to buy them alive, taking care not
to kill them till just before cooking. The heaviest are the best; and
if the tail strikes quick and strong, they are in good condition, but
if weak and light and frothing at the mouth are exhausted and
worthless. In like manner, when buying a boiled lobster put your
finger and thumb on the body and pinch it; if it feels firm, and
the tail goes back with a strong spring, the lobster – if heavy and of
a good colour – is a desirable specimen.

These instructions are given by the cookery expert of *Spons Household Manual*, published in the eighties. Nowadays lobsters, except
for restaurants, are nearly always bought ready cooked, but, while
nobody can be blamed for avoiding participation in the martyr's
death they die, the fact remains that a freshly cooked lobster prepared in one's own kitchen makes a very much better dish than
one cooked by the fishmonger. It may be of some solace to know

that Mr Joseph Sinel, who made experiments on behalf of the R.S.P.C.A., came to the conclusion that a lobster put into cold water which is slowly brought to the boil collapses and dies painlessly when the heat reaches 70°.

BOILED LOBSTER

'Lobster is, indeed, matter for a May morning,' said Peacock, 'and demands a rare combination of knowledge and virtue in him who sets it forth.' He would no doubt have considered this dish of lobster, simply boiled and served piping hot, a suitable morsel for breakfast.

Tie up the tail of the lobster to the body with string (the fishmonger will do this for you) and put it into a large pan of cold salted water. After it has come slowly to the boil, cook it for 20–30 minutes according to the size. Take it out of the pan, clean the scum off the shell and rub it over with a little butter or oil. Break off the claws, crack them carefully at each joint so that they come to pieces easily, cut the tail down the middle and leave the body whole. Put all on to a large hot platter and serve with melted butter or a *sauce tartare*.

BUTTERED LOBSTER

For six people you need 3 medium-sized cooked lobsters. The tails are cut in half and put under the grill for a few minutes with a little butter. The rest of the meat is cut into dice, seasoned with salt, pepper, a dash of cayenne and a generous sprinkling of lemon juice; heat this in a sauté pan with butter, shaking the pan to prevent the lobster from sticking. Serve in a heap in the centre of the dish with the tails arranged round, garnished with quarters of lemon.

Crawfish, or *langouste*, are not so common in England as lobster, but when they do appear they are cheaper and, in the opinion of many people, more delicate. They have no claws, and sometimes the tails only are sold.

LANGOUSTE À LA GRECQUE

Cut 2 medium-sized onions in thin slices, sauté them until golden in a small wineglass of olive oil; then add ½ lb of chopped tomatoes and stir in for a few minutes. Season with salt, pepper and a handful of chopped parsley, then pour in a glass of white wine. Let it cook fiercely for a few seconds. At this stage put in the cut-up pieces of *langouste* and let the pan simmer until the sauce attains a fairly thick consistency. The dish can be served hot, or cold, when it makes a rich hors-d'œuvre.

HOMARD À LA CRÈME

1 cooked lobster, ¼ lb mushrooms, 4 oz cream, 1 liqueur glass each brandy and pale sherry, 2 oz butter, lemon juice, salt and pepper, cayenne pepper.

Melt the butter in a shallow pan and put in the pieces of lobster, seasoned with the salt, pepper and lemon juice. When the butter is foaming, pour in the brandy and set it alight, and as soon as it has finished burning add the mushrooms cut in thin slices, the sherry and a suspicion of cayenne. Stir the contents of the pan for 2 or 3 minutes and pour in the cream. Another 5 minutes over a moderate flame and the lobster is ready. This a simple and delicious dish which is too often spoilt by the addition of tomato sauce, too much sherry and a thickening of flour and milk.

When cream is not available, milk can be used and the sauce bound with the yolk of an egg at the very last minute – do not let the sauce boil after you have added the egg.

Beware of poor quality sherry: I have known even a little ruin the dish with its overpowering flavour, and, failing a reasonably good dry or medium sherry, twice the quantity of white wine can be used.

LANGOUSTE EN BROCHETTES

For each person allow 1 medium-sized crawfish tail, a rasher of bacon, 2 oz of mushrooms, half a tomato, lemon juice, a little butter.

Cut the cooked meat of the crawfish tail into squares, and each rasher of bacon into about 6 pieces. Sauté the mushrooms for 2 or 3 minutes in a little butter. Put a half tomato on to a skewer, cut side towards the point. Then thread on the crawfish, the bacon and the mushrooms alternately until the skewer is full. Melt the butter in a pan and pour it over the skewers, the contents of which have been seasoned with a little salt, pepper and lemon juice.

Put the skewers on to the toaster, over a fireproof dish, and cook under the grill, turning them once and basting with the butter as you do so. Cook them 5–7 minutes, until they are hot.

Arrange them on a dish, garnished with bunches of watercress and halves of lemon. With them serve either of the following sauces: hot melted butter in which there is a squeeze of lemon juice and some cut-up chives; or fresh cream whipped with a scrap of salt and pepper and mixed with chopped tarragon, served very cold.

LANGOUSTE À LA CATALANE

Into a ready prepared *All Grenat* or *Bouillade* sauce (pp. 171–2) put the flesh of a cooked crawfish or lobster, cut into small squares and seasoned with black pepper and lemon juice. Simmer 3 or 4 minutes only, until the lobster is hot.

LANGOUSTE DE L'ÎLE SAINTE MARGUERITE

Cold, freshly boiled crawfish or lobster is served with an accompaniment of hot, crisp, fried onions, cooked as described for the *Paillettes d'Oignons* on pp. 144–5.

Indigestible but delicious.

SCALLOPED OYSTERS À LA CRÉOLE

Into individual buttered fireproof dishes, put a layer of bread-crumbs mixed with a little chopped parsley, chopped tomato, a suspicion of chives and cayenne pepper.

On this bed place 6 or 8 oysters for each dish, another layer of the breadcrumb mixture, and some butter in small pieces.

Fill the dishes up with cream and the liquor from the oysters, and bake in a medium oven for 5 or 6 minutes.

SHRIMPS À LA CRÈME

Butter some shallow individual china dishes, and into each one put 2 tablespoons of peeled shrimps (or prawns). Cover the shrimps with thin cream, a fine sprinkling of breadcrumbs, a knob of butter on the top, and put in a medium oven (Gas 5) for 6 or 7 minutes, until they are just turning brown on the top.

ESQUINADO À L'HUILE

Esquinado is the Provençal name for the Spider Crab.

The crab (a female one is preferable, for the eggs improve the taste of the dish) should be cooked for 30 minutes in water to which is added a few drops of vinegar, salt, 2 or 3 peppercorns and 2 bayleaves.

When cold, take out all the inside including the eggs and the flesh from the claws, and pound it in a mortar, with the yolks of 2 hard-boiled eggs, a teaspoon of dry mustard, the juice of a lemon, salt and pepper. Put the purée through a fine sieve into a basin. Add gradually about 1 gill (5 oz) of olive oil, so that the purée is well amalgamated, and finally a little finely chopped parsley.

The purée is served in the crab shell, the outside well cleaned and rubbed over with a little olive oil.

To be served as a sauce with any plainly cooked white fish, with risotto, hard-boiled eggs or as an hors-d'œuvre with slices of toasted French bread.

SCALLOPS FRIED IN BATTER

For the batter:

¼ lb flour, 3 tablespoons olive oil, a pinch of salt, ¾ tumbler tepid water, 1 white of egg.

Sieve the flour, mix in the olive oil, the salt, and the water. Leave the batter to rest for at least 2 hours. When ready to use, stir in the beaten white of egg. This amount will make about 24 fritters.

Cut 12 scallops into two rounds each. Reserve the coral. Season the scallops with salt, pepper and lemon juice. Dip each one in batter and fry in very hot, but not boiling, deep fat or oil. Drain them on a paper napkin.

Warm the coral in a little butter and garnish the dish with them, and alternate quarters of lemon. Alternatively the slightly cooked coral can be pounded and added to a mayonnaise, but the taste of these scallop fritters is very delicate and they do not really need a sauce.

MUSSELS

Allow about 1 pint of mussels per person and 1 pint over — there are nearly always a few which have to be discarded. Put them into a bowl of cold water, covered with a damp cloth over which you strew a little coarse salt. Leave them in a cold place for 2 or 3 hours. This process helps to clean them.

When you are ready to cook them throw away any which are opened or broken, and put the rest in a basin of clean water under a running cold tap. Scrape, scrub and beard each one separately, putting them into a second basin of cold water while you do so. When they are thoroughly cleaned, leave them another 10 minutes in a colander under the running tap, then in cold water again for a further 10 minutes. All this sounds very complicated, but it is most important to remove all grit and sand.

The mussels are now ready to cook, and whether they are to be served *à la marinière*, *au gratin*, as a garnish, in a salad or an omelette, soup, risotto, or fried in batter, the preliminary method is the same, but the cooking medium differs.

For *moules marinière* they are cooked and served in their shells in a *court-bouillon* of water and white wine or white wine only with chopped shallot and parsley, for *moules poulette* the same *court-bouillon* is thickened with egg yolks while the mussels are kept hot in another dish. For soups and risottos the method is as for *marinière*, the stock being used as a basis for the soup or to cook the risotto in, and the mussels shelled. If to be served in a *gratin*, the mussels can be cooked in very little water, white wine, or cider, for a salad or hors-d'œuvre in olive oil; when the stock or oil in which they have been cooked is to be used again for the sauce, soup, or risotto, it is strained through a muslin, as there is always a little sediment at the bottom, however carefully they have been cleaned.

The method of cooking them is as follows: put the water, the wine, or the olive oil in a wide pan, put in the mussels and cook them on a moderate flame until they open, moving them round from time to time with a wooden spoon so that the top ones get cooked at the same time as those underneath. The process takes about 10 minutes, and when they are opened they are ready. Often there are one or two which refuse to open and these can be left a little longer after the others have been taken out. Overcooking shrivels them up and spoils them. Salt can be added when they are cooked; sometimes they are salty enough, but it is impossible to tell beforehand.

MOULES À LA BORDELAISE

Clean the mussels, allowing 6 pints for four people; let them open over the fire with a glass of white wine. Strain them and remove the empty half-shell.

In a small pan melt 1 oz of butter, and in this sauté 2 chopped shallots; add 1 lb of tomatoes cut up, seasoning, a clove of garlic, a handful of chopped parsley and one of breadcrumbs which have been soaked in milk to soften them and then strained; stir the sauce until the tomatoes are cooked, then add a little of the strained juice from the mussels, and a teaspoon of grated lemon peel. Put the mussels into a gratin dish, pour the sauce over them and simmer for 3 or 4 minutes, until the mussels are hot.

Messy to eat, but a dish with character.

MOULES NIÇOISES

For four people you need about 6 pints of mussels; this amount should give about 18 mussels per person, allowing for those which are open or broken and have to be thrown away. Clean them as explained on pp. 40–1, and put them into a wide shallow pan with a glass of white wine or cider; let them open by rapid boiling, removing them the very minute they are opening; they are to be cooked again, so they must not be allowed to dry up. Strain the wine in which they have cooked through a muslin.

Prepare a *Pestou* (p. 171) with butter, and substituting parsley if there is no fresh basil available. Remove the empty half-shell from each mussel and put the remaining half-shells with the mussels in them into individual metal or china egg-dishes, about eight inches in diameter.

Spread a little of the prepared *Pestou* on to each mussel, moisten with a few drops of the strained stock and put the dishes under the grill to melt and brown the sauce, 3 or 4 minutes for each dish.

MOULES AU GRATIN

First prepare 2 oz of butter pounded with a clove of garlic and some finely chopped parsley. With an oyster knife open the cleaned, uncooked mussels, at least a dozen per person; put a little of the prepared butter on each mussel, arrange them in a fireproof dish and heat them until the butter is melted.

Pour a cup of fresh cream mixed with about 3 tablespoons of grated Parmesan cheese over them and put them in a hot oven or under the grill to brown.

GRATIN OF MUSSELS, MUSHROOMS, AND SHRIMPS

4 or 5 pints mussels, ¼ lb mushrooms, ½ pint cooked shrimps, 1 glass white wine, 2 oz cream, breadcrumbs, 1 small clove of garlic, parsley, 1 oz flour, 1 oz butter.

Clean the mussels, put them to cook in ½ pint of water and the white wine. When they are opened strain them, keeping the stock. Shell the mussels. Strain the stock through a muslin. Make a white *roux* with the butter and flour, add the strained mussel stock and cook until it is smooth. Now add the cream and the mushrooms, previously sautéd a minute in butter, and the shrimps. When the sauce is thick and creamy, stir in the mussels. Turn the mixture into a fireproof gratin dish, well buttered.

Add a little cut parsley, a handful of breadcrumbs, some nuts of butter and put under the grill until golden and bubbling.

LAITANCES AU VIN BLANC

Soft roes are cheap, plentiful, and can be cooked in a few minutes. They are usually served as a savoury, but are better as a first dish.

Butter a shallow dish, lay the roes in it, and on top 2 chopped tomatoes, a scrap of grated lemon peel, salt, pepper, parsley and a little more butter. Pour over ½ wineglass of white wine, cover with a thin layer of breadcrumbs and cook in the oven for about 10 minutes.

MACKEREL EN PAPILLOTES

Choose fairly small mackerel, one for each person, and have them split and cleaned. For four, prepare a mixture of a teacup of chopped parsley, ½ teacup of capers, 2 oz of butter, a strip of lemon peel, a pinch of cayenne, salt and black pepper. If you can get fennel, add ½ teacup of the chopped leaves to the mixture — fennel is particularly good with mackerel — and knead all the ingredients together.

Put a portion of this mixture inside each mackerel. Butter 4 squares of greaseproof paper, put a mackerel on each one, and fold over the edges so that no butter can escape. Lay them on the grid in the preheated oven, as you would a baked potato, and cook (Gas 4) for 25–30 minutes, putting the ones which have to go on the lower shelf into the oven 5 minutes before the others.

To serve them, turn them out of their paper cases into a hot dish with all the butter and herbs poured over them, and accompanied by slices of lemon. No sauce or vegetable is necessary, but they must be very hot. The mackerel can be prepared in their papillotes beforehand, and even if they are left a little longer than necessary in the oven they will come to no harm.

FILETS DE MAQUEREAUX GRATINÉS AUX CÂPRES

Arrange your fillets of mackerel in a flat buttered fireproof dish; salt and pepper them and pour over a small glass of white wine. Cover and cook in the oven.

In the meantime, melt a nut of butter in a saucepan; stir in a spoonful of flour; let it cook a minute and add stock made from the bones of the fish. The sauce should be smooth and creamy, but not too thick. Add a beaten egg and stir again without letting the sauce boil; now add a tablespoon of capers, and pour over the fillets. Sprinkle breadcrumbs on top, and a little melted butter, and put the dish under the grill to brown, but only for two or three minutes or the sauce will curdle.

GRILLED MACKEREL

Make two slanting incisions, on each side of the cleaned mackerel. Into these put a little butter worked with parsley, pepper and salt, fennel, and a few chopped capers. Put the mackerel under the grill with a fireproof serving dish underneath. Grill them 7–10 minutes on each side; add a squeeze of lemon juice to the butter in the dish. No other sauce is necessary, for the mackerel will be quite delicious cooked in this simple way.

Herrings, mullet, whiting and trout can be grilled in the same way.

FILETS DE MAQUEREAUX AU VIN BLANC

One of the classic hors-d'œuvre of France, but very rarely met with in England.

Prepare a *court-bouillon* with a wineglass of white wine and one of water, an onion, a clove of garlic, a bayleaf, salt and ground black pepper, and a piece of lemon peel. Bring this to the boil, let it cook 5 minutes, then leave it to cool.

Put the cleaned mackerel into the cold *court-bouillon* and let them cook very gently for about 15 minutes; leave them to get cold in the *court-bouillon*. Split them carefully, take out the bones, remove the skin and divide each fish into about 6 or 8 small fillets, and arrange in a narrow oval dish. Reheat the *court-bouillon*, letting it bubble until it is reduced by half. When it is cool, strain it over the mackerel, and garnish the dish with a few capers and some chopped chives or parsley.

STUFFED BAKED HERRINGS

Have the herrings boned; stuff them with a smooth, creamy purée of potatoes, flavoured with pepper and nutmeg and fresh herbs. Wrap them in buttered paper, place them on the grid in the oven and cook at a moderate heat for about 10 minutes.

They can also be cooked under the grill on an electric stove.

TURBOT À L'ESPAGNOLE

Put a sliced onion to brown in a little olive oil; add 1 lb of tomatoes, roughly chopped, and seasoning of salt, pepper, sugar, sweet basil, a clove of garlic and a dessertspoon of paprika pepper. Cook slowly until it is almost a purée.

In the meantime poach a fine whole turbot in a *court-bouillon* to which you have added a wineglass of white wine, cider or sherry, an onion, a bayleaf, a piece of lemon or orange peel, salt and pepper. When the fish is cooked, drain it carefully and put it on the serving dish. Add a wineglass of the *court-bouillon* to the tomato sauce and go on cooking until it is well amalgamated. Pour the sauce over the turbot, and when it is cold garnish with lemon peel and some green herbs — either tarragon or chives.

Turbot should be cooked the day it is to be eaten and not too long beforehand; it loses its delicacy if left more than an hour or two.

TURBOT NORMAND

First prepare 3 pints of *Moules Marinière* (p. 41) and take them out of their shells. Pour the liquid from the mussels through a muslin. In the meantime slice 5 or 6 onions and sauté them in butter, so that they melt and turn almost to a purée.

Put the onions into an oval fish dish, pour over the liquid from the mussels, put the turbot on the top and add a tumbler of cider. Cover the pan and cook in the oven, basting the fish with the liquid from time to time. When the turbot is cooked, add a lump of butter which has been mashed with a little chopped parsley and a drop of lemon juice, put the mussels all round and leave the dish in the oven just long enough for the mussels to get hot.

A handful of fresh shrimps added to the garnish is an improvement.

SOLE AU VIN BLANC

For four people:

8 fillets of sole, ¼ bottle white wine, not too dry, 4 oz cream, 1 oz flour, tarragon, 1 oz butter.

Roll the fillets up and place them in a buttered fireproof dish. Season them with salt and pepper and pour the wine over them. Put a sprig of tarragon into the wine. Cover the pan, and put it in a moderate oven (Gas 4) for about 10 minutes.

In the meantime, make a white *roux* with the butter and flour, and while this is cooking put the cream into a small pan and simmer it for 3 or 4 minutes until it has reduced and thickened. Add it slowly to the flour-and-butter mixture, stir it well, and then put it aside while you remove the sole from the oven, pour off the wine in which it has cooked into another small pan, and keep the fish covered and warm in the bottom of the oven. Let the wine simmer until it has reduced by half; you can tell by the delicious aroma coming out of the pan when it is ready. Now add this slowly to the cream sauce, stirring over a very low fire, and cooking for 3 or 4 minutes until it is the right consistency. If too thick, add a little more cream; if too thin, then cook a little longer.

Now pour the sauce (through a sieve if it is at all lumpy) on to the fillets, add a tablespoon of chopped tarragon, a fine dusting of breadcrumbs, a knob of butter, and put under a hot grill to brown.

This really is a delicious creamy dish, and one of the few ways of cooking sole in which the richness of the sauce does not detract from the natural flavour of the sole.

CHEESE SOUFFLÉ WITH FILLETS OF SOLE

The yolks of 4 eggs and the whites of 5, 2½ oz grated cheese, preferably equal parts of Gruyère and Parmesan, salt, pepper, 1 oz butter, 4 fillets sole.

Roll up the fillets of sole, seasoned with salt and pepper, and cook in a buttered dish in the oven for 5 minutes. They do not need to be quite cooked, as they are cooked again in the soufflé.

Butter a soufflé dish and place the fillets at the bottom, well drained of any liquid that comes from them while cooking. Separate the eggs. Beat the cheese into the yolks until the mixture is creamy. Whip the whites very stiffly, fold them into the yolks, pour quickly into the soufflé dish and put it straight into a pre-heated oven (fairly hot). Cook for 12–15 minutes.

The timing of soufflés is entirely a matter of experience and depends upon practice and the knowledge of one's own oven, so that while Gas 7 is the set temperature for soufflés on my own gas cooker, the pressure varies considerably in different districts and according to the age of the stove. So before venturing upon a soufflé for a dinner party, it is wise to carry out a few experiments, noting the time taken and the temperature of the oven for the most successful.

ROUGET FLAMBÉ AU FENOUIL

In the market-places of Provence they sell bunches of fennel stalks specially for *les grillades au fenouil*. There is no substitute, but fennel is easy enough to grow in any garden or in pots.

Clean out the red mullet, but leave in the liver. In the opening put 2 or 3 stalks of fennel. Put them in a bed of dried fennel branches, cover with melted butter and put under the grill.

When they are done on both sides, withdraw the dish from the grill. Pour over a glass of Armagnac and set light to it. Bring the dish to the table while the Armagnac is still burning.

COLIN À L'OSEILLE

Colin is another name for merluche or hake. Saithe or rock salmon can also be used for this dish.

Sorrel is not often seen in England, although I have managed to buy it in London from time to time, and some enterprising people grow it in their gardens.* It has a delicious flavour, rather acid, and is a perfect foil for fish and eggs.

For *Colin à l'Oseille*, poach a large piece of hake or rock salmon in a *court-bouillon* with an onion, herbs, and lemon peel.

Clean the sorrel (about 1 lb), and cook it as for spinach, with as little water as possible. Make this into a purée by putting it through a sieve, mix in 2 yolks of eggs, a little French tarragon mustard, a few leaves of raw sorrel which you have reserved, chopped finely with a few leaves of tarragon.

Serve the fish on this green bed, either hot or cold, garnished with lemon. A fine summer dish.

LE BROCHET AU BEURRE BLANC DE VOUVRAY

You need a pike weighing not less than 2 lb and the following vegetables and herbs:

A sliced onion, a sliced carrot, a sprig of thyme and one of fennel, a bayleaf, parsley, salt, 2 or 3 peppercorns.

Bring all this to the boil in about 1 pint of water and a glass of white wine, and then leave it to cool. Put the cleaned fish in, bring it to the boil again, and let it poach for 20 minutes.

In the meantime, prepare your *beurre blanc*. In about 5 oz of white wine (in Touraine they naturally use the wine of Vouvray, but any light white wine of Anjou would do, or even a Pouilly) put 6 finely chopped shallots, and 3 tablespoons of the *court-bouillon* of the fish. Reduce this over a gentle fire to a fifth of its original volume, then add little by little 6 oz of butter which you have already

* The nursery gardens mentioned on page 133 sell sorrel plants.

worked a little with a fork to soften it, and 1 oz of fresh cream. Whatever happens, the sauce must not boil, or disaster will ensue. (It would be wise to do this sauce, after the preliminary reduction of the wine, in a bowl over a pan of hot water.)

Beat continuously with an egg whisk so that the butter 'rises' and froths; season with salt if necessary. The sauce must be ready at the same time as the fish is cooked, and must be served immediately.

Accompany this splendid dish with plainly boiled potatoes and the same wine as you used for the sauce.

'It is with tears of gratitude in their voices,' writes the author of this recipe, 'that your guests will remind you of the *beurre blanc de Vouvray*.' Another version of *beurre blanc* is made simply with the butter and shallot mixture, without cream.

Pike is fairly rare in England. It is quite possible to make this dish with a small turbot, a fine whole sole, or a salmon trout.

CARPE À L'OSEILLE

A carp weighing 3 lb, salt, pepper, 4 lb sorrel, 6 hard-boiled eggs, 3 onions, thyme, bayleaf, 2 oz butter.

Put the carp, very well cleaned, into a pan containing a tumbler of water, the 3 onions sliced, salt, pepper, thyme and bayleaf, cover it, and cook in a medium oven for about 30 to 40 minutes.

Cook the sorrel in a little water, drain it and leave it *en branche*, mixed with the butter. Take the carp out of the oven and put it on a hot dish surrounded by the sorrel and the hard-boiled eggs cut in halves.

LA BOURRIDE

Bourride is almost as popular a dish in Provence as the *Bouillabaisse*. It is easier to achieve away from the Mediterranean than *Bouillabaisse*, for it does not require any special fish like the *rascasse*, and its success depends on the sauce, which is a feast for anyone fond of garlic.

You require about three different kinds of white fish, such as bass, gurnet and sea bream. Clean them and cut them into thick slices.

Prepare a *court-bouillon* with water, a little white wine, vinegar, onion, bayleaf, orange peel and fennel and the heads of the fish. Bring this to the boil, cook it 10 minutes, and let it cool.

Now prepare an *aïoli*, that is to say, a mayonnaise with garlic. The garlic, say 2 large cloves for four people, is pounded in a mortar, 2 yolks of eggs stirred in, then the oil added drop by drop at first, and faster as the *aïoli* gets thick. For *Bourride* you will need at least ½ pint of *aïoli*. When it is ready, put the prepared fish into the *court-bouillon* and poach it for 10–15 minutes. Prepare 2 slices of toasted French bread for each person and put them into a warmed fish dish.

In a double boiler put half the *aïoli* and stir into it 2 or 3 yolks of eggs, then through a strainer a ladle of the *court-bouillon* from the fish. Stir this, without allowing it to boil, until it is thick and creamy. Pour it over the toast, arrange the drained fish on the top, and serve the rest of the *aïoli* separately.

At the Voile d'Or in St Raphael, famous for its *Bourride*, they serve a *Sauce Rouille* as well as the *aïoli*. This is made not in the usual way with breadcrumbs, sweet peppers, and olive oil but with the grilled, skinned red peppers pounded into the *aïoli*, plus pounded lobster coral and the pink inside of *oursins*, Mediterranean sea urchins. They also serve a green sauce made of a particular kind of seaweed cooked and pounded into the *aïoli* with a flavouring of *Pastis*, or *Pernod*, which gives it an aniseed flavour.

A simpler kind of *Bourride* can be made with one large fish such as bream, cooked whole, and one sauce, the *aïoli* mixed with the extra eggs, and the stock from the fish.

CATIGAU D'ANGUILLES

A very old Provençal recipe, given by Madame Léon Daudet, in *La France à Table*, January 1935.

In a sauté pan put a little olive oil with a few strips of bacon, and let them turn very lightly brown. Next add about 1 lb each of sliced onions and 1 lb of the white part of leeks cut in rounds. Let these brown slightly and then add 1 lb of tomatoes cut in pieces and 3 or 4 cloves of garlic crushed, a bayleaf, salt, pepper, and a good pinch of saffron. On top of this put a layer of sliced raw potatoes and the eels* cut in thick slices. Add water or white veal stock to cover.

Boil rapidly for 20 minutes, and season with a good measure of freshly ground pepper from the mill before serving. Pour the stock from the *catigau* over pieces of French bread in a deep dish and serve the eels and vegetables on another dish.

MATELOTE OF RIVER FISH
(as it is made on the banks of the Seine)

You will need a carp, an eel and, if you can get it, a tench.

Scale and clean the carp carefully, remove the gills and the head and cut it in thick slices; you can either skin the eel or not, as you like, but in any case cut the head off and cut the rest in slices, as also the tench, and roll each slice in flour.

In the meantime, in a large pan, put 20–25 small onions to brown in butter; add a tablespoon of flour and a little water or stock; stir it, and see that it does not get too thick. Now pour into the pan a pint of red Vin Ordinaire, salt, pepper, a *bouquet garni* composed of thyme, bayleaf, parsley and a clove of garlic all tied together.

When the onions are half cooked, add the pieces of fish; cook for 5 minutes, pour in a small glass of cognac, and set light to the sauce; when the flames have gone out, cook another 20 minutes on a fairly brisk flame.

Serve the *Matelote* on slices of toasted French bread and garnished

---

* If you prefer to cook the eels without their rather oily skins, first put the slices into cold water, and as soon as it boils strain the eels. The skin will then come off easily.

with quarters of hard-boiled egg. The sauce should be creamy but not too thick.

This is the simple and genuine *Matelote*, and it is excellent.

TROUT IN ASPIC

Make a *court-bouillon* with a large glass of white wine, an onion, garlic, a few rounds of carrot, herbs and seasoning, 1 pint of water and the head of any white fish.

Let this cool, then put in the cleaned trout. Poach them gently until they are cooked, lift them out of the pan and arrange them in a long, fairly deep dish.

Reduce the *court-bouillon*, adding seasoning if necessary but no salt, until the end. This stock is to be poured through a muslin over the fish and should set to a light jelly; decorate with a few leaves of tarragon or some slices of lemon.

BOUILLINADA

This is one of the Catalan versions of *Bouillabaisse*.

Into a wide copper or heavy sauté pan put a tablespoon of pork or bacon fat. Add a cupful of parsley chopped with 3 or 4 cloves of garlic and a red pimento cut into strips. When this has cooked a minute add a layer of raw, thinly sliced potatoes, then a layer of thick slices of fish such as bass, whiting, sea bream and John Dory.

Now another layer of potatoes and fish until it is all used up. The proportions of potatoes and fish should be about equal; about 2½ lb of each for six people (it is not worth making any kind of *Bouillabaisse* for less than six people, owing to the different kinds of fish required). Add water up to the top of the fish and potatoes, but don't actually *cover* them.

Cover the pan, bring it very quickly to the boil, add 2 table-spoons of olive oil, put the lid back again and cook it very fast for about 15–20 minutes. The rapid boiling will amalgamate the liquid and thicken it, giving the dish its own particular savour. Serve very hot in heated soup plates.

A few carefully cleaned mussels, put on the top of the last layer in the pan, and served as they are, in their shells, are a good addition to this Catalan *Bouillabaisse*.

TUNNY FISH WITH SAUCE TARTARE

A small tunny fish is cooked whole in a *court-bouillon*, as you would cook a salmon, allowing about 15 minutes to the pound. Drain the fish and leave it all day on a wire sieve or other strainer which will accommodate it comfortably, in order that the fat may drain off.

The fish can then be put into the refrigerator and served very cold next day with a *Sauce Tartare*.

Slices of fresh tunny can be cooked in the same way.

EGGS

EGGS

POACHED EGGS

This is what Dr Kitchiner, author of the *Cook's Oracle* (1829) has to say about poached eggs: 'The cook who wishes to display her skill in Poaching, must endeavour to procure Eggs that have been laid a couple of days, those that are quite new-laid are so milky that, take all the care you can, your cooking of them will seldom procure you the praise of being a Prime Poacher: You must have fresh Eggs, or it is equally impossible.

'The beauty of a Poached Egg is for the yolk to be seen blushing through the white – which should only be just sufficiently hardened, to form a transparent Veil for the Egg.'

My own method for poaching eggs I learnt from a cookery book published by the Buckinghamshire Women's Institute, and it has proved infallible.

First boil a saucepan of water, and into this dip each egg whole, in its shell, while you count about thirty, then take it out. When it comes to actually poaching the eggs, have a pan of fresh water boiling, add a dessertspoon of vinegar, stir the water fast until a whirlpool has formed, and into this break the eggs, one at a time. 1–1½ minutes cooks them. Take them very carefully out with a draining spoon. They will be rounded and the yolks covered with a 'transparent Veil' instead of the ragged-looking affair which a poached egg too often turns out to be, and the alternative of the egg-poaching pan, which produces an over-cooked sort of egg-bun, is equally avoided.

It is interesting to note that Dr Kitchiner instructs his readers to place poached eggs on bread 'toasted on one side only'. How right he is; I have never been able to understand the point of that sodden toast . . .

Try serving poached eggs on a piece of fresh, buttered bread; alternatively on a purée of some kind – split peas, sweet corn, or mushrooms, with pieces of fried bread around, but not under, the egg.

ŒUFS BÉNÉDICTINE

Poached eggs served in individual flat dishes, over which you pour a tablespoon of Hollandaise sauce. Originally the eggs were placed on a bed of creamed salt cod (*brandade de morue*) but nowadays are more often served on pastry or croûtons.

ŒUFS MOLLETS AUX FINES HERBES

These can be made either with poached eggs or *Œufs Mollets* or coddled eggs — that is, eggs put in boiling water and boiled for 4–5 minutes, steeped in cold water and shelled. The white is cooked and the yolk soft without being runny.

Allow 2 coddled eggs per person, a dessertspoon of fresh chopped herbs such as parsley, chives, and tarragon and a tablespoon of butter. Melt the butter, put in the eggs and sauté them without letting the butter burn. Sprinkle in the herbs and a squeeze of lemon juice, and serve immediately.

This is one of those excessively (and deceptively) simple dishes which can make the reputation of a good cook; the process only takes about 2 minutes, so provided that the eggs are prepared beforehand and the herbs ready chopped, they can be made at the last minute.

They are nicest cooked and served in individual metal eggdishes.

EGGS EN COCOTTE

Have your little fireproof china dishes ready with a good lump of butter in each, and an egg for each person ready broken into a separate saucer. Put the little dishes into the oven (Gas 5) and take them out as soon as the butter has melted, slide an egg into each, pour a large tablespoon of cream on to the egg, avoiding the yolk, return them to the oven. They will take 4—5 minutes to cook, allowing perhaps ½ minute less for those on the top shelf.

If you leave them too long, the yolks get hard and the dish is ruined, so be on the alert to see that they are taken out of the oven at the exact moment.

Experience and knowledge of the idiosyncrasies of one's own oven are the mediums of success here. No pepper or salt should be added, except at table, but a very little cut fresh tarragon when they come out of the oven is an acceptable addition.

ŒUFS À LA MONTEYNARD

4 eggs, ½ lb rice, 4 tablespoons grated Gruyère cheese, 1 tumbler of good stock, 1 oz fresh butter, salt and pepper.

Boil the rice in the usual way, but for only 10 minutes, drain it and then put it on to cook again with the stock, simmering it slowly.

In the meantime, put the eggs into boiling water and let them boil five minutes, no longer. Take them out and put them in cold water.

Shell them. Butter a fireproof dish. Into this put the rice, which should have absorbed all the stock and be quite cooked. With the back of a spoon make eight indents in the rice, to hold the 8 half eggs. Cut the eggs very carefully in half (if they have been boiled properly the yolks should still be slightly runny). Put them into the places you have made for them; season the eggs and the rice with a sprinkling of salt and pepper then add the grated cheese, putting a double layer on each half egg.

Pour the melted butter over the dish, which then goes into a hot oven for not longer than 3 minutes, so that the yolks of the eggs will remain soft under their coating of *gratin* formed by the butter and the cheese.

FROMAGE D'ŒUFS À LA MAYONNAISE

Break the eggs whole into a large, well-buttered dish or mould. Place this in a *bain-marie* filled with water and cook until the eggs have set.

When they are cold, turn the eggs out whole on to a round dish, mask them with a well-flavoured thin mayonnaise, and garnish with a mixture of chopped chives, parsley and tarragon.

RAGOÛT OF MUSHROOMS AND EGGS

Put about ½ lb of mushrooms into a pan with a little water, bring them to the boil and add I gill of white wine. Season with salt, and a discreet amount of ground black pepper, nutmeg and herbs.

Let the *ragoût* boil again for 2 or 3 minutes; and meanwhile have hot in a dish 5 or 6 hard-boiled eggs, roughly chopped, and a few plainly grilled whole mushrooms.

Pour the *ragoût* over the eggs, garnish with the grilled mushrooms, and serve at once.

An excellent dish, either to start the meal or as the vegetable course after cold meat or game, or as a main luncheon dish.

PIPÉRADE

Pipérade is the best known of all Basque dishes, and various recipes for it have appeared in English cookery books. It is a mixture of sweet peppers, tomatoes, and onions, with eggs added at the end; the final result is a creamy scrambled-egg effect deliciously blended with the vegetables in which the sweet pepper flavour slightly dominates. Sometimes one meets it with the purée of onions, tomatoes, and peppers topped with fried eggs, sometimes in the form of an omelette; the scrambled-egg version is the most characteristically Basque.

1 lb onions, 1 lb tomatoes, 3 fairly large sweet red peppers or about 6 of the small green ones, in season in the Basque country long before the red ones, 6 eggs.

In a heavy frying or sauté pan melt some pork fat (sometimes olive oil is used for this dish, but pork, or even bacon fat, suits it better). Put in the sliced onions, and let them cook slowly, turning golden but not brown: then put in the peppers, cut into strips; let this cook until it is soft, then add the chopped tomatoes, with a seasoning of salt, ground black pepper and a little marjoram. Cook with the cover on the pan.

When the whole mixture has become almost the consistency of a purée, pour in the beaten eggs, and stir gently, exactly as for ordinary scrambled eggs. Take care not to let them get over-cooked.

With the *Pipérade* are served slices of the famous *Jambon de Bayonne*, most of which is in fact made at Orthez, in the Béarn.

The *Jambon de Bayonne* is something like the Italian *Prosciutto* and imparts its particular flavour to many Basque and Béarnais *garbures* and *daubes*. Brochettes of calf's liver are sometimes served with the *Pipérade* and a very good combination it is.

ŒUFS MARITCHU

Another Basque dish.

For each person allow 1 artichoke, or 2 if they are small, 2 eggs, and 1 lb of tomatoes for four people.

First cook the artichokes in boiling water for 20–30 minutes, and when they are cool, take off all the leaves, leaving only the heart. Sauté them gently in butter or oil, and in the meantime have ready the sauce made with fresh tomatoes, chopped with an onion and a clove of garlic and simmered in a covered pan; the sauce can be used as it is or put through a sieve.

When the artichokes and the sauce are ready, put them into a serving dish, the artichokes in the centre and the sauce all round, and on top of each artichoke put about 2 tablespoons of very creamy scrambled eggs.

OMELETTE AUX POMMES DE TERRE

The best potato omelette is made with potatoes cooked as for *Galette de Pommes de Terre* (p. 137). When the *galette* is ready add a little butter to the pan and let it run round the edges; pour in 4 or 5 beaten eggs and shake the pan so that the eggs cook; turn the omelette out flat, like a Spanish *tortilla*.

Another method is to grate I oz Gruyère cheese into a cup of cream and pour it over the omelette as soon as the eggs have set, making a rich but still simple dish.

OMELETTE AUX CROÛTONS ET FROMAGE

In butter fry a handful of little squares of bread; keep them hot on a plate.

Pour the beaten eggs for the omelette into hot butter in the omelette pan, put in the croûtons, then 2 tablespoons of grated cheese. Fold the omelette over quickly and slide it on to the hot dish.

The combination of the cheese and the croûtons of bread is particularly good.

FONDUE DE FRANCHE COMTÉ

Put ¼ pint of white wine into a saucepan with a chopped clove of garlic and cook until the wine is reduced by half. Strain it and leave to cool.

In a bowl beat 6 eggs with ½ lb of grated Gruyère cheese, 2 oz of butter, some ground black pepper and a little salt. Stir in the reduced wine and pour the mixture into an earthenware or other fireproof dish and stir over a low fire until the mixture forms a creamy mass, well amalgamated, but in no way resembling scrambled eggs.

Serve at once in the pan in which it has cooked, and boiling hot. Each person should have a supply of squares of bread or toast; with a fork these are dipped into the *Fondue*, which gets increasingly good as the bottom of the dish is reached. Sufficient for 4 or 5 people. This *fondue* is distinct from the Swiss *fondue*, in that the Swiss one is made without eggs, and with the addition of Kirsch.

LUNCHEON, SUPPER
AND FAMILY DISHES

LUNCHEON, SUPPER AND FAMILY DISHES

It is more often when planning day-to-day meals, with ingredients forced upon one by circumstances rather than specially ordered for a grand occasion, that the general provider and cook is hard put to it to think of something new to put before the family, and at the same time not waste food which may already be in the house. Most of the soups in this book come into the category of dishes which can be made according to whatever ingredients may be most easily obtainable; in this chapter I have endeavoured to suggest a few more out of the ordinary ways of presenting such things as liver, dried vegetables, potatoes, cabbages, and sausages, as main dishes. This is the kind of food which is eaten frequently in thrifty French households, and it is very good.

If we all had cooks (and butchers) such as the charming character described below by Edmond About, I suppose life would be very much easier, but then we shouldn't get quite so much satisfaction out of inventing some excellent dish out of practically nothing at all.

I must tell you that in 1845 (I am speaking of a long while ago) the servants were part of the family itself. They lived for so long in the same house that people fell into the habit of calling them by the surnames of their masters. Angélique, ladies' maid to the three daughters of the pork butcher, was known as Angélique Fondrin, and the old bewhiskered coachman who drove the mayor's carriage answered locally to the name of Léonard Morand. My worthy Catherine, still in my service, as I am in hers, was at that time a strapping young woman of thirty-four. My parents had taken her on when she was very young, she had grown up with us, she had become accustomed to us, without a teacher she had mastered the fine art, so French and at the same time so rare in France, of roasting a leg of mutton to a turn, of fricasséing a chicken, of the discreet seasoning of a *salmis* of partridge or woodcock. She could knead a potato cake before which a professional pastry cook would have gone on bended knees. Rice, which every housewife of Courcy reduced to a nauseating glue, was transformed, on her stove, into golden beads of an exquisite flavour. She excelled above all at simple dishes, and the tax collector, a worthy man whose friendship had followed us into the uppertown, used to say that Catherine's *Bœuf aux Choux* was as good as a truffled turkey at the Crown. At the time of our comparative prosperity the worthy creature was cited as a model of delicacy; the wits of the club claimed that, to avoid temptation, she had had the handle of her shopping basket removed.* But, after our ruin reduced her wages to practically nothing, her probity turned into cunning and sorcery; for us she would have stolen the fairy queen's wand. Molière's miser would have found his ideal in this girl, who borrowed bones from the best butcher in Courcy to make *consommés* and jellies for my mother. Both butchers' and household bones were bought indiscriminately, at the same price, by a travelling rag and bone man. Every week Catherine took away fifteen or twenty kilos of beef bones and returned them to the butcher's boy after having extracted a jar of fat and a mountain of jellied stock by long boiling. This cost her a few *sous*, a small pie made by herself, or simply a handshake. The fat which she obtained in this way was better than butter, and made excellent *friture*.

This culinary imagination, the desperate pursuit of good value, and the everlasting search for free nourishment which resembled the mediaeval alchemist's dream of the philosopher's stone, did not always come off. She suffered some singular failures, notably with *Choucroûte*, which always turned out to be a very expensive dish, and the famous Tripe vaunted by Rabelais. It can scarcely be imagined how much care and time, how much bacon and spice are needed to succeed with this Pantagruelish dish which our ancestors, the ancient Tourangeaux, ate until it gave them indigestion.

Catherine was sincerely wretched at not being an accomplished *cordon bleu*; she would ask me why the Minister of Education (M. le Comte de Salvandy, if I remember rightly) did not found a school

* A play on the expression *'faire danser l'anse de son panier'* — to cheat one's employers.

of cooking in every town, simply in order to conserve the meat and vegetables which everywhere went to waste, to the detriment of the public's nourishment. And perhaps the good girl was right. But even in her mistakes and mishaps she was the object of envy of every housewife in the neighbourhood. If ever she were to write her memoirs, like M. de Talleyrand, a rather less irreproachable cook, she could reveal the flatteries, the promises, and the intrigues of five or six noble ladies who would not have shrunk from crime in order to prise her away from us. Provincial life is subject to these ferocious comedies.

Le Roman d'un brave homme
by Edmond About

FOIE DE PORC BRAISÉ

In a 2 to 3 lb piece of pig's liver make a number of small incisions in rows, and in these put small pieces of bacon rolled in ground black pepper.

Place 4 or 5 rashers of bacon in a casserole and on these put the liver; pour over enough white wine and stock or water in equal quantities to come up to the level of the liver; add 6 carrots, an onion stuck with a clove, a bayleaf, thyme, parsley, a few peppercorns and a crushed clove of garlic. Put another rasher or two of bacon over the top of the liver, cover the casserole and simmer in the oven for about 30 minutes.

Strain off the sauce, remove the excess fat, and put the sauce into a small saucepan to reduce by half; when it is thick enough, add a walnut of fresh butter, pour over the liver, and serve quickly.

FOIE DE VEAU EN BROCHETTES

Buy the calf's liver in one piece, and cut it into pieces about an inch wide and quarter of an inch thick. Season them with salt, pepper and marjoram, and a drop of lemon juice.

Have the same number of small pieces of bacon. Thread the liver and bacon alternately on skewers. Pour a few tablespoons of olive oil on to a dish and roll the skewers in the oil. Grill them, not too fast, for about 7 minutes, turning them over once.

Serve them on the skewers on a bed of vegetable purée such as celery, or lettuce, or potato, or buttered rice (p. 73), or *Pipérade* (pp. 60–1).

LIVER AND BACON PÂTÉ

For six people:

1 lb liver sliced, 6 rashers bacon, ¼ lb mushrooms, thyme, lemon peel, garlic, pastry, sherry, or port, or white wine.

Sauté the liver gently in good dripping or butter. Add the mushrooms sliced, and when they have cooked a minute or two pour into the pan whatever wine you are using and let it reduce by half.

In a small terrine, or pie-dish, put a layer of chopped bacon, then a layer of the liver mixture, seasoned with salt, pepper, a very little garlic, thyme and lemon peel, another layer of bacon, and so on until it is all used up. Cover with a crust of pastry, stand in a pan of water, and bake in a moderate oven.

This can be eaten hot or cold, and can also be done without the pastry crust, in which case cover it with a buttered paper and the lid of the terrine.

ROGNONS AU MAÏS

In south-western France maize is cultivated in great quantity; the pigs and geese are fed on it; the country people have a host of dishes, both sweet and savoury, made from maize flour, which is similar to Italian *Polenta*. Tinned sweetcorn makes quite a good substitute for some of the savoury dishes. The purée should be made as thick as possible.

1 lb kidneys, 1 oz dripping, 1 tin sweetcorn (the plain, not the creamed, variety), 1 oz butter, salt and pepper, 1 cup milk or meat stock.

Remove the skin and the fat from the kidneys and blanch them in boiling salted water. Drain them, cut them in slices and sauté them for 10 minutes in the dripping.

Have ready a purée made from the tinned sweetcorn, simmered in the milk or stock, and put then through the sieve twice. This double sieving is always necessary with sweetcorn, or it will not be smooth enough.

Heat up the purée with the butter, put it on a hot dish and arrange the kidneys on top.

GNOCCHI À LA ROMAINE

Although generally supposed to be an Italian dish, these *gnocchi* are also a speciality of the Nice district; having been part of Italy for so long, the cooking of the *Pays Niçois* has much in common with that of Genoa, and it is hard to say exactly where dishes such as this actually originated.

1 pint milk, 4 oz semolina, 3 oz grated cheese, salt, pepper, nutmeg, 1 tablespoon marjoram and chives, butter, an egg.

Bring the milk to the boil in a double saucepan, with salt, pepper, nutmeg, marjoram and chives. When the milk boils, put the semolina in, and stir it until the mixture has about the consistency of porridge, and a wooden spoon will stand up in it.

Take it off the fire and stir in the beaten egg, 1 oz of cheese and 1 oz of butter. Pour the mixture into a buttered tin and spread it out about a quarter of an inch thick and leave it to cool. Cut it into rounds about the size of a half-crown, arrange them overlapping in a generously buttered gratin dish, put more butter on the top and the rest of the grated cheese. Heat under the grill, slowly to start with, until the *gnocchi* are warmed through, then faster to brown them.

If you have some good meat glaze, or chicken *velouté*, a little poured over the *gnocchi* just before you take them from the grill is most delicious. *Pestou*, a basil and garlic sauce pounded with olive oil or butter and Parmesan cheese, also goes particularly well with *gnocchi*. The recipe is on p. 171.

QUICHE LORRAINE

For six people:

6 oz flour, 2 oz butter, 1 oz lard, 6 rashers bacon, ½ pint cream, 2 fresh eggs, salt and pepper, ½ gill water.

Make a pastry with the flour, the butter, the dripping, a pinch of salt and the water. Give it two or three turns and then roll it into a ball and leave it for 1 hour.

Line a flat buttered pie-tin with the rolled-out pastry. On to the pastry spread the bacon cut into dice and previously fried for a minute. Now beat the 2 eggs into the cream with a little salt and ground pepper; when they are well mixed, pour on to the pastry, put it into a hot oven at once and bake for about 30 minutes.

Let it cool a little before cutting and serving.

LA QUICHE AUX POMMES DE TERRE

Cook 4 large potatoes in their skins, and when they have cooled put them through a sieve and mix them with 2 tablespoons of flour, 2 oz of butter, and salt until you have a compact paste. Roll it out a quarter of an inch thick and spread it in a floured and greased flan tin. Prick the paste here and there with a fork. Fill up the potato tart with a mixture of small pieces of bacon (about 2 rashers) and 4 oz of good fresh cream. Season with a scraping of nutmeg and a very little garlic. Sprinkle the top with grated Gruyère cheese. Put into the oven (Gas 6) for about 20 minutes.

This dish is best served cold, and is excellent for a picnic. If you have to make do with thin cream or top of the milk, mix it with the yolks of 2 eggs.

BUTTERED RICE

A simple way of serving rice as an accompaniment to chicken or meat dishes, or by itself with a bowl of grated cheese.

Boil the rice in the usual way — that is, allowing 2 oz per person, put into a very large pan of boiling salted water, into which you have also put half a lemon. Boil for 15 minutes, drain very carefully, and dry in a warm oven for 2 or 3 minutes.

Stir into the rice a beaten egg and 1 or 2 oz of butter; a few chopped chives make a pleasant addition.

MACARONI AU JUS DE VIANDE

This is a dish to be made when there is good meat stock left over from a *daube* or from a stewed duck. The macaroni, or spaghetti, 2 or 3 oz per person, should be put into a very large pan of boiling salted water and cooked for 15 minutes, or until it is tender.

Have ready a warmed fireproof dish, and put the drained spaghetti into this; stir in a breakfast cup of good thick stock (previously reduced, if necessary), a lump of butter, some freshly chopped herbs such as parsley, basil, and chives and some grated Parmesan. Stir over the fire for a minute or two so that the spaghetti is hot. Serve more grated cheese separately.

Good either alone or as an accompaniment to a meat dish.

TARTE AUX ASPERGES

For the pastry:

½ lb plain flour, 6 oz butter, a pinch of salt.

For the filling:

A 2-lb bunch of asparagus, ¾ pint béchamel *sauce made with milk or cream, 2 oz grated cheese.*

Knead the flour and butter together, adding a little water to make a paste. Prepare this 1 hour before cooking, if possible.

Prepare the asparagus very carefully, peeling off the dry outer skin of the stalks. Put them tied in a bunch and heads uppermost into boiling salted water, to which you add also a lump of sugar and cook them for 20 minutes (a little longer if they are very large ones). Drain them and cut each asparagus into 3 or 4 pieces, discarding the hard part at the ends.

Roll out your pastry, line a flat buttered pie-tin with it, cover the inside and the edges with kitchen paper and put the usual beans into the paper to keep the pastry flat. Bake it in a hot oven for 20 minutes. Now add the grated cheese to the prepared *béchamel* and, off the fire, the asparagus.

Take the paper and the beans off the pastry, fill up with the asparagus mixture, put it into the oven to brown, and serve very hot.

CROQUETTES DE VOLAILLE

These croquettes can be very good if well made, crisp on the outside and creamy within; they can be made with left-over chicken, but not in the slapdash way usually reserved for 'remains'.

For four people you need:

6 oz chicken without skin or bone, 2 oz ham or bacon, a sheep's brain (this helps the croquettes to attain the required smoothness), an onion, 3 or 4 mushrooms chopped, a béchamel *made from 1 oz butter, 1 oz flour, ⅓ pint milk. For cooking the croquettes — an egg, breadcrumbs, and deep fat.*

If possible, prepare the mixture beforehand, and do the final operations the next day. Melt the butter, put in the finely chopped onion and let it cook without browning, add the ham or bacon, minced, then the flour and the milk, a little salt, pepper, and a pinch of nutmeg. Stir until the sauce is smooth and let it reduce by nearly half.

Blanch the sheep's brain and chop it with the chicken and the mushrooms; add this mixture to the sauce, give it 2 or 3 minutes over the fire and pour it out into a dish, smoothing down the surface.

The next day take a tablespoon at a time of the mixture and roll it in your hands, floured, to the right shape. Dip each croquette first in beaten egg, then in fine breadcrumbs, in the egg again, and lastly the breadcrumbs. This double egg-and-breadcrumbing makes a good coat for the croquettes, so that the hot fat crisps them but does not penetrate the inside.

Drop each croquette in the hot deep fat; they should be cooked in 2–3 minutes; drain them carefully and serve them on a napkin, accompanied, if you like, by a sauce, tomato, mushroom, or Béarnaise.

TARTE À L'OIGNON

In nearly every French province, but particularly in Alsace-Lorraine, there are recipes for onion tarts, sometimes made with a purée, sometimes with fried onions, green spring onions, leeks. Some people add bacon, some cream. In Provence the equivalent is the *Pissaladina*, where the already cooked onions are baked on bread dough and garnished with black olives. The recipe I am giving here is from Lorraine.

Make a short crust with 8 oz of flour, 4 oz of butter, a pinch of salt and a little water. Leave it to rest while preparing 1½–2 lb of sliced onions; melt them gently in butter, bacon fat, or beef dripping. This will take about 30 minutes, with the pan covered. Take them off the fire, and stir in 2 beaten eggs, and 2 oz of grated Gruyère cheese. Roll out the pastry, spread it on the tart tin, fill up with the onion mixture and bake it in a moderate oven for 20 to 30 minutes.

SAUCISSES AUX PISTACHES

For 2 lb of pork sausage meat, well seasoned with salt, pepper, and 2 cloves of garlic, you need 4 oz of pistachio nuts. Put in a pan and pour boiling water over them. After 15 minutes the skins will rub off. Chop them finely, or pound them in a mortar, and add them to the sausage meat, with the yolks of 2 eggs. Fill the sausage skins with the mixture.

To be fried or grilled.

LE SAUCISSON CHAUD AU VIN

There are many ways of treating sausages with wine and many varieties of sausages with which to do it. This recipe is best for the uncooked coarsely cut type of sausage, such as the *Saucisse de Toulouse*, which can be bought from Aubin in Brewer Street, Soho, or else for the Italian *Zampone* or *Cotechini*, to be found at Camisa & Son in Old Compton Street or Parmigiani's in the same street, and in good Italian provision shops in many other London districts. Smoked sausages of the Frankfurter type can also be used, or the Polish sausages now sold in many delicatessen shops.

Make a *court-bouillon* with 4 carrots, 2 onions, the white part of 2 leeks, a small turnip and 2 tomatoes, all cut up finely. Put all these into a pan, add 2 or 3 branches of any one rather strong herb, either basil, rosemary or thyme, a bayleaf, a branch of parsley, a very little salt and two crushed peppercorns, and pour over them ½ pint of red or white wine and ¼ pint of water. Let this cook until the vegetables are half done.

Make a few small incisions here and there in a sausage weighing about 1 lb and poach it in the *court-bouillon* for 40 minutes. Serve it in its own liquor, accompanied by potatoes or white haricot beans. Cider can be used instead of wine.

LE CASSOULET DE CASTELNAUDARY

Je veux vous amener chez Clémence, une petite taverne de la rue Vavin, où l'on ne fait qu'un plat, mais un plat prodigieux. On sait que pour avoir toutes ses qualités le cassoulet doit cuire doucement sur un feu bas. Le cassoulet de la mère Clémence cuit depuis vingt ans. Elle ajoute de temps en temps, dans la marmite, de l'oie, ou du lard, parfois un morceau de saucisson ou quelques haricots, mais c'est toujours le même cassoulet. La base demeure, et c'est cette antique et précieuse base qui donne au plat une qualité comparable à ces tons ambrés si particulier qui caractérisent les chairs dans les œuvres des vieux maîtres vénitiens.

So wrote Anatole France of the *Cassoulet*, wonderful dish of south-western France, which through the years has been raised from the status of a humble peasant dish to one of the glories of French cooking. Toulouse, Carcassonne, Périgord, Castelnaudary, Gascony, Castannau, all have their own versions of the *Cassoulet*. The ingredients vary from fresh pork and mutton to smoked sausages, garlic sausages, bacon, smoked ham, preserved goose or pork, duck, calves' feet, the rind of pork and pigs' cheek. The essentials are good white haricot beans and a capacious earthenware pot (the name *Cassoulet* comes from Cassol d'Issel, the original clay cooking utensil from the little town of Issel, near Castelnaudary).

For the *Cassoulet* of Castelnaudary the ingredients are:

1½–2 lb medium sized white haricot beans (this amount will feed six to eight people; the Cassoulet *is a dish to be made in quantity; it can be heated up), a wing and a leg of preserved goose (p. 114) or half a fresh goose, a coarse pork sausage of about 1 lb or several small ones,* ½ lb bacon, 3 onions, 4 or 5 cloves of garlic, 2 tomatoes, and, if possible, 2 pints of meat stock.*

Put the beans to soak overnight; next day put them into fresh water and cook for about 2½ hours, keeping them just on the boil, until they are three-quarters cooked, then strain them.

In the meantime prepare the stock in which they are to finish cooking. Slice the onions and cut the bacon into squares and melt them together in a pan, add the crushed garlic, the tomatoes, seasoning and herbs, and pour over the stock and let it simmer for 20 minutes. Take the pieces of goose out of their pot with the good lard adhering to them. (If you are using fresh

---

* See preceding recipe for places where these sausages may be bought.

goose, it must be half roasted; have some good pork or goose dripping as well.)

Put the goose, the dripping, the sausage, and the bacon from the stock, at the bottom of the earthenware pot, which has been well rubbed with garlic, and the beans on the top. Add the prepared stock. Bring the *Cassoulet* slowly to the boil, then spread a layer of breadcrumbs on the top and put the pot into a slow oven and leave it until the beans are cooked. This will take about 1 hour, during which time most of the stock will be absorbed and a crust will have formed on the top of the beans.

Serve exactly as it is; a good young red wine should be drunk with this dish; a salad and a country cheese of some kind to finish will be all you need afterwards.

Duck can be used instead of goose, and at Christmas the legs or wings of a turkey go very well into the *Cassoulet*.

BACON AND LENTILS

Put 1½ lb of farmhouse bacon into a saucepan, cover it with cold water, bring it to the boil, strain it, rinse it in cold water and dry it in a cloth.

Melt a little dripping in a deep casserole, put in the bacon and a dozen or so small onions, with a seasoning of ground black pepper. When the onions begin to turn brown, add 1 lb of brown lentils, a carrot cut in two, a stick of celery, a bunch of fresh herbs tied together, and 2 or 3 crushed cloves of garlic. Cover with water, put the lid on the casserole, and cook very slowly for about 2 hours.

When the lentils are cooked take out the bacon, remove the carrot and the bunch of herbs, and strain the lentils. Put them on the serving dish with a lump of butter stirred in, arrange the bacon cut in slices all round and garnish with chopped parsley, and, if they are available, some halved hard-boiled eggs.

Sufficient for six people.

LA TRUFFADO

This is a peasant dish from the Auvergne, made with *fromage de Cantal*, which is something like English Cheshire cheese, which can be used instead, but it must be real Cheshire, not processed cheese, which will not melt.

Slice 1 lb of raw potatoes thinly and cook them in a frying-pan as for the *Galette de Pommes de Terre* (p. 137), with the addition of a few small dice of bacon and a clove of garlic finely chopped. When the potatoes are almost cooked add the cheese, about 2 oz, cut in very small pieces, and turn the potatoes once or twice so that the cheese spreads all over them.

Cover the pan, turn the fire off, and leave the cheese to melt in the heat of the pan for 5 minutes before serving.

EL PA Y ALL

The breakfast dish of the Catalan peasants in the Roussillon district of France ... A piece of bread fresh from the baker (or sometimes fried in oil or pork fat) is rubbed all over with a piece of garlic, as little or as much as you like; then sprinkled with salt, then a few drops of fresh olive oil, and the *Pa y All* is ready.

STUFFED CABBAGE
DISHES

To show what can be done with a cabbage apart from the one
and only, and far too notorious, way common to railway dining-
cars, boarding-schools and hospitals (and, goodness knows,
these are all places where we should be offered the maximum of
consolation in the way of good food), I am giving several recipes,
each with its regional characteristic, for turning cabbage into an
acceptable main-course dish, inexpensive, but abounding in the
rich aromas of slow cooking and careful preparation.

There is a choice of two Provençal recipes, a dish using game,
red cabbage served with smoked sausages, and a Catalan stuffed
cabbage with pimentos and black olives. There are many more
such recipes, but anyone can evolve their own from the ingredients to hand.

All these dishes are admirable for Aga and other cookers of
the same type. They can be left in the slow oven for hours, and
forgotten until dinner-time.

CHOU FARCI AUX CÂPRES

A fine large cabbage, about 6 oz each of minced fresh pork or pure pork sausage meat, chicken livers, and breadcrumbs, 1 yolk of egg; seasonings, spices, herbs; a roux made of 1 oz butter, 1 oz of flour, ½ pint stock or tomato juice; 2 tablespoons of capers, 1 small glass of brandy.

Put the whole cabbage into boiling, salted water and let it blanch for 5 minutes; take it out, drain it, and, placing it on a wooden board, unfold the cabbage leaf by leaf, until it looks like an open flower. Now carefully spread each leaf with the stuffing made from the pork, the chicken livers, the breadcrumbs, all finely minced and amalgamated, bound with the yolk of egg and seasoned with salt, pepper, a little powdered thyme or marjoram, a clove of garlic, nutmeg, and a minced bayleaf. When all the stuffing is used up, press the leaves of the cabbage gently together and tie it into its original shape with tape.

Have ready in a deep earthenware dish a *roux* made from the flour, butter and stock. Into this put your cabbage, stud it with 4 whole cloves, cover the pot and put it into a slow oven (Gas 2 or 3) for about 2 hours.

When the cabbage is cooked, take the tape away very carefully and transfer the cabbage with its sauce to a deep serving dish, strew it with the capers and finally pour the brandy over it.

GROS CHOU FARCI À LA PROVENÇALE

For this version of the stuffed cabbage, the stuffing consists of the meat from a pork cutlet, 1 oz of lean bacon, ¼ lb of beef, veal or chicken meat, a sheep's brain, 2 eggs, a few lettuce leaves, 2 oz of grated Gruyère cheese, an onion, a clove of garlic, and rice.

Mix all these ingredients together (finely chopped) and add a cupful of cooked rice. Put the stuffing into a pan with a little olive oil and let it cook for 1 or 2 minutes.

Meanwhile blanch the cabbage, then separate the leaves, cutting out the hard part and adding the heart, finely chopped, to the stuffing. Spread the leaves with the stuffing, tie up the cabbage and put it into a casserole with some carrots cut in rounds, sliced onions, garlic and shallots, a branch of thyme, a bayleaf, and salt and pepper.

Pour over a tumbler of white wine and one of water or stock, cover the pan, and simmer very slowly for 3–4 hours, moistening the top of the cabbage from time to time with its own juice.

CHOU FARCI À LA MODE DE GRASSE

Once upon a time the *Chou Farci*, or *Sous Fassoun* in Provençal, was the great speciality of the town of Grasse. Here is the old recipe; a dish for the hungry, but no longer a cheap one.

Put a large white cabbage into boiling water for 5 minutes. Drain it, and carefully separate the leaves.

Have ready a stuffing composed of 2 oz of uncooked rice, 2 oz of pure pork or veal sausage meat, 3 oz of salt pork (or green bacon), ½ lb of minced pig's liver, ½ lb of fresh peas, the heart of a lettuce, the white part of 2 leeks, finely chopped, and 2 egg yolks.

Mix all the ingredients in a large bowl, bind the stuffing with the yolks of eggs, and season with salt, pepper, mace, nutmeg, a crushed clove of garlic and herbs. Spread each cabbage leaf with the stuffing, laying them one on the other until you have used up all the leaves and the stuffing. Tie the cabbage up with tape.

Line a deep casserole with slices of lean beef or veal, squares of raw ham or salt pork, a pig's trotter,* 6 carrots and turnips and a *bouquet garni* of thyme, parsley, rosemary and a bayleaf. Put the cabbage in the centre, pour over a tumbler of stock or water, cover the pan and cook extremely slowly in the oven for 2 or 3 hours.

Serve the cabbage in the centre of a big dish, the meat and vegetables all round, and a tomato sauce separately.

* If the pig's trotter has been salted, soak it for several hours, before cooking, in warm water.

CHOU FARCI CATALAN

This dish is made with the remains of beef which has been cooked in a *pot au feu*, a *bœuf à la mode*, or the *Estouffat* (pp. 93–4), or the mutton from the *Daube Avignonnaise* (p. 91).

About 4 oz meat, 2 oz bacon or ham or salame sausage, 3 or 4 sweet red or green peppers, 12 black olives, ½ oz dried cèpes or mushrooms, 2 or 3 cloves of garlic, seasoning, mace, marjoram, bayleaves, fat bacon, a little of the stock or sauce from whatever meat is being used, 1 egg, 2 small cabbages.

Chop the meat with the bacon, a sweet pepper from which all seeds have been removed, the black olives and garlic, season with salt and pepper (if the olives are salt add very little to the mixture), and the mace, nutmeg and herbs, and stir in the egg. Put the dried mushrooms to soak in a little warm water for 10 minutes.

Put the cabbages whole into boiling salted water for 5 minutes. Strain them, and when they are cool open out the leaves, putting the stuffing in between, until it is all used up. Fold the leaves back again until the cabbages are as nearly as possible their original shape. Tie them carefully round with tape. Place the cabbages in a deep earthenware pot into which they just fit (one for each cabbage, if necessary), slice the 3 remaining peppers into strips and place them with the dried cèpes round the cabbages. Put thin slices of the bacon on the top, pour a ladle or two of the sauce or stock over the cabbages (water, if no stock is available), cover with a greaseproof paper and the lid of the casserole and cook in a slow oven (Gas 2 or 3) for 3 hours.

To make a more substantial dish, almost any kind of sausages can be added half-way through the cooking, or some home-cured bacon or ham.

The nicest accompaniment to this rustic dish is not potatoes or any vegetable, but a few slices of bread gently fried in the dripping from whatever meat has been used.

CHOU FARCI CHASSEUR

Blanch the cabbage, drain it, and cut out the stalk. Spread out the leaves and in between each put a mixture of cooked chestnuts, chopped smoked sausages (Frankfurters) and the meat of a cooked partridge, pheasant, or 2 pigeons, or some roast hare. Season with salt, pepper, herbs, nutmeg and mace.

Tie the cabbage up, put it into a casserole, and moisten it with a tumbler of white wine and one of game stock. Simmer with the lid on the casserole for about 3 hours.

The proportion of stuffing for all these dishes is 16–18 oz for a 2½–3 lb cabbage.

CHOU ROUGE LANDAIS

1 medium-sized red cabbage, 1 lb cooking apples, 1 lb onions, 2 smoked Frankfurter sausages per person, ¼ pint red wine, 1 gill wine vinegar, 4 tablespoons brown sugar, herbs and seasoning, 2 sweet red peppers, garlic, a piece of dried orange peel.

Slice the cabbage crosswise into thin strips. Peel, core, and slice the apples, and slice the onions.

In the bottom of a deep casserole put a layer of cabbage, then one of onions, then apples. Season with salt, pepper, sugar, herbs, mace, ground cloves, garlic, and add the strips of raw sweet pepper and dried orange peel. Continue these layers until the casserole is full up. Moisten with the wine and the vinegar. Cover the casserole and cook in a very slow oven for 3–4 hours. 20 minutes before serving add the sausages, buried deep into the cabbage.

The aroma which emanates from the cooking of this dish is particularly appetizing.

To make the dish more substantial, a few thick slices of bacon can be added. A bacon or ham bone, or even bones from roast mutton cooked with the cabbage and removed before serving, enrich the flavour.

MEAT

MEAT

When visiting Paris or any large provincial town in France it is an education to watch the housewives doing their meat marketing and to see the butchers at work, preparing a fillet of veal for roasting, or larding a piece of beef for a *bœuf mode*; for in France the butcher does all this for you, and you are not required to explain how the veal must be cut for *escalopes*, or for *blanquette de veau*, or fillet of beef for *tournedos*, and if you wish a *gigot* or shoulder of lamb to be boned it will be done without fuss or argument. Recently, Harrods of Knightsbridge have opened a French butcher's shop where nearly all the French cuts may be bought straight off the counter, and if what you need is not on show, it will be done to order.

It is much to be hoped that this innovation will eventually have widespread effects on our meat marketing in this country, for in the end it is more economical to pay a little more for expertly cut and trimmed meat than to buy it cheaply and cut it inexpertly at home. Most particularly does this apply to the cheaper cuts.

VEAU AUX TOMATES

A piece of roasting veal, fillet for preference, weighing 2–3 lb, 12 tomatoes, 12 small onions, garlic, shallots, herbs.

Put 2 cloves of garlic inside the veal, rub it all over with salt and pepper, and brown the meat in olive oil or dripping. Turn the flame down and add the whole skinned tomatoes and the whole small onions, 2 chopped shallots, a branch of rosemary and seasoning. Cover the pan and let the meat cook gently, without any water; there should be enough moisture from the tomatoes, but should the pan get dry add a few spoonfuls of meat or vegetable stock.

Serve the veal on the bed of onions with the tomatoes all round.

ESCALOPES DE VEAU SOPHIE

Have your *escalopes*, 1 or 2 for each person, beaten out very thin and flat, seasoned with salt, pepper and lemon juice. For each *escalope* have a thin slice of ham or bacon and half a hard-boiled egg. Lay the ham on the meat and the half egg on top. Roll up each *escalope* and tie it with thread.

Cook them in butter for 10 minutes, then add a glass of cream and simmer for a few minutes more in the covered pan.

ESCALOPES DE VEAU EN PAPILLOTES

4 escalopes of veal, 4 slices ham, ½ lb mushrooms, 2 onions, parsley, 2 oz butter.

Beat the *escalopes* out thin, season with salt, pepper and lemon juice, fry them very lightly on each side in butter. Take them out of the pan, and in the same butter fry the finely chopped onions and mushrooms; stir in a handful of chopped parsley; spread this mixture on to the *escalopes* and on top of the mixture place the slice of ham.

Now cut a large heart-shaped piece of greaseproof paper for each *escalope*; butter one side of it and place the veal and ham on it. Fold it over and turn down the edges so that no juices can escape. Heat them in a slow oven for about 20 minutes.

The nicest way to serve them, if your guests don't mind getting their fingers messy, is piled up in the dish in their paper bags, so that none of the aromas have a chance to evaporate until the food is ready to be eaten.

ROGNONS DE VEAU AUX TOMATES

Skin the kidneys and soak them in warm salted water to clean them. Put them into a pan with good dripping, and ¼ lb of bacon for 2 lb of veal kidneys. Let them roast very gently for about 20 minutes.

In the meantime brown a dozen or so chopped shallots in bacon fat or beef dripping; add 1 lb of tomatoes chopped, seasoning of salt, pepper, basil or marjoram, a lump of sugar and a glass of port, or sweet white wine, or cider. When this has cooked for 10 minutes, add ½ lb mushrooms, and the kidneys and bacon. Cook for another 10 minutes.

This dish can be served quite alone, or with a *galette* of potatoes.

NAVARIN PRINTANIER

This is a *ragoût* of lamb or mutton to which spring vegetables give special character.

Cut 2 or 3 lb of shoulder or breast of lamb into squares. In a large, shallow, sauté pan put 2 or 3 tablespoons of good dripping or butter. In this put 3 small sliced onions, then add the pieces of meat, and when they are golden take them out and put them on a plate; to the dripping in the pan add 2 tablespoons of flour, and stir until you have a light brown *roux*. To this add about 1 pint of brown stock (vegetable stock made with fried onions, carrots and the usual soup vegetables will do) and go on stirring until the sauce has amalgamated. Put back the meat, season with salt, black pepper, a sprig of rosemary, a crushed clove of garlic and a bayleaf. Simmer with the lid on until the meat is nearly cooked – about 1 hour – but this depends on the quality of the meat.

Now add 1 lb of new potatoes, a small bunch of new carrots, and a few baby turnips; cook slowly for another 35–40 minutes and then add 1½ lb of green peas, freshly shelled; as soon as they are cooked the *Navarin* is ready. If the sauce gets very reduced during the cooking add more stock or water; it should be neither very thick nor very thin; about the consistency of a cream soup.

GIGOT AUX FLAGEOLETS OU AUX HARICOTS

This is a standard dish of many Paris *bistros*, and it is excellent if mutton and beans are both cooked *à point*.

Roast the leg of mutton, with a clove of unpeeled garlic underneath it and several sprigs of rosemary strewn over it, in good dripping.

The *flageolets*, or white haricot beans, should be soaked the night before; they will take about 3 hours to cook, well covered with water, with an onion and a bayleaf, salt and pepper. Simmer them until they are soft; this should coincide with the moment the *gigot* is cooked. Remove the *gigot* to a large fireproof serving dish, strain the fat from the roasting-pan.

Add a little white wine to the juice in the pan, a little water, and let this bubble a minute. Pour this gravy over the strained beans, and put them all round the *gigot*. Put into the oven for a few minutes, adding a lump of butter to the beans before serving.

Tinned green *flageolet* beans are very good and can be used for this dish; they need only be heated for 10 minutes.

SELLE D'AGNEAU BASQUAISE

Roast a saddle of lamb in the usual way, with a clove of garlic underneath it in the pan, and in the meantime brown some whole, small, raw potatoes in goose dripping; they must be cooked slowly, in a heavy pan on top of the stove, or else be baked in a covered pan in the oven at the same time as the meat; they will take about 40 minutes to 1 hour, according to size.

While these are cooking, prepare the almonds, about 2 oz, which must be skinned and chopped, but not too finely; 10 minutes before serving add them to the potatoes and keep an eye on them to see they don't burn. Lastly, prepare a *Sauce Béarnaise* to which you add finely chopped mint instead of the usual tarragon.

Serve the saddle of lamb surrounded by the potatoes and almonds, and the sauce separately.

DAUBE À L'AVIGNONNAISE

4 lb leg of lamb or mutton, 4 large onions, 2 or 3 carrots, ½ bottle of red wine, salt, pepper, herbs, 4 cloves of garlic, a piece of orange peel, 4 oz of fat salt pork or bacon, a handful of parsley, 1 small glass of brandy, olive oil.

Cut the meat into fair-sized pieces, each weighing about 3 oz. Into each piece of meat insert a small piece of salt pork or bacon which has been rolled in the parsley chopped with a clove of garlic. You will need about 1 oz of the 4 oz of pork or bacon.

Put the prepared meat into an earthenware dish with 2 onions, and carrots cut up, salt, pepper, and herbs (thyme, bayleaf, marjoram). Pour the red wine over, and the brandy, and leave to marinate 4 or 5 hours.

Into a heavy stewpan put the rest of the pork cut in squares and 4 or 5 tablespoons of olive oil, and let the bacon melt a little in the oil. Now add the other 2 onions, sliced, and let them brown, then put in the pieces of mutton, with some fresh herbs and seasoning, the orange peel and 3 cloves of garlic. Pour over the wine in which the meat has marinated and let it bubble until it has reduced by about one-third. Just cover the meat with boiling water. Put the lid on the pan and simmer very slowly for 4–5 hours.

The *daube* can be made the day before it is wanted, any surplus fat skimmed off the sauce when it is cold, and gently reheated. A few stoned black olives and a ½ oz of dried cèpes added before the water is put in add to the very southern flavour of the *daube*.

The nicest accompaniment is a dish of dried white haricot beans, cooked with a piece of salt pork and a garlic sausage, and moistened before serving with some of the sauce from the *daube*.

CHÂTEAUBRIAND EN TERRINE

Into an earthenware terrine with a lid pour a glass of dry white *vin ordinaire*, a glass of Madeira, and a liqueur glass of brandy and put this to heat gently on a low flame.

Now slice 2 or 3 small onions, the same number of carrots, and sauté them very lightly in a little butter. In the same butter sauté on each side your beef, which should be a fine piece of *filet*, thick and in one piece, weighing 1½ to 2 lb, seasoned with salt and black pepper.

By this time the contents of the terrine should just be beginning to simmer; place the beef in this liquid, cover it with the carrots and onions, and add a chopped shallot, a suspicion of garlic, 4 fine tomatoes, peeled, and each cut into eight pieces.

Now cover the terrine and seal the lid with a flour and water paste. Place the terrine in a very slow oven (Regulo 1 or 2) for 2 hours. Serve in the dish in which it has cooked.

The juice of the *Châteaubriand*, mingled with the wines and the vegetables, will give forth the most wonderful aroma when you finally open the dish.

You can, if you like, accompany the meat with a very light purée of potatoes.

I can assure you,' says Albert Chevallier, the author of this recipe, 'that kings and princes have feasted like gods on this dish, although it is a simple, bourgeois household dish, albeit a gourmet household.'

A persuasively written recipe — but not one to be taken too literally. Fillet steak cooked for two hours, even in the slowest of ovens, will be reduced to rags. Best, therefore, to simmer the sauce with its carrots, onions, tomatoes and wines for at least an hour before putting in the beef. After its initial browning, 45 to 50 minutes with the terrine or casserole placed low down in the slowest possible oven will then be sufficient.

PAUPIETTES OF BEEF

8 thin slices of beef cut from the round, without fat and each weighing approximately 1 oz, 2 oz of bacon and mushrooms, 1 egg, 2 onions finely chopped, 1 tablespoon French mustard, 1 clove of garlic, 1 dessertspoon finely chopped lemon peel, 1 tablespoon breadcrumbs, flour, dripping, salt and pepper, thyme, a handful of parsley.

Fry the onions, mushrooms and bacon in a little dripping, then mix in the lemon peel, breadcrumbs, parsley and seasoning, and a beaten egg.

Flatten out each slice of beef; season with pepper, salt and thyme. On each slice lay a little heap of stuffing, roll up the meat and secure with a tooth-pick, or tie with string. Roll them in flour and brown them in dripping, in a small sauté pan. Add water just to cover, and simmer very slowly for 30 minutes. Now with the point of a knife crush a small piece of garlic and add this to the sauce, together with the French mustard, and cook for another 30 minutes. The sauce should be creamy and piquant. The dish can be made beforehand and heated up.

Serve with either boiled rice or a purée of potatoes.

A WINE MARINADE FOR MEAT

In a saucepan heat a wineglass of olive oil; when it is hot put in a sliced carrot, one sliced onion, and half a head of celery cut in inch lengths.

Let these vegetables brown lightly and pour in ¼ pint of white wine and a small glass of wine vinegar. Add 4 or 5 stalks of parsley, 4 shallots, 2 cloves of garlic, thyme, bayleaf, a sprig of rosemary, 6 peppercorns and salt.

Simmer this for 30 minutes. Leave it to cool, and then pour it over your piece of meat.

L'ESTOUFFAT DE BŒUF

This is the Gascon way of doing beef *en daube*, and is one of the traditional dishes eaten in Gascony on Christmas Eve. It is cooked in an oval earthenware casserole.

You need:

1½ lb fresh rind of pork (this is used in many soups and ragoûts in France, but can be replaced with a pig's foot), herbs, 7 or 8 shallots, 2 large onions cut into four,

1 or 2 carrots, 6 lb topside of beef in one piece tied into a sausage shape, 2 claret glasses of Armagnac or brandy, a half-bottle of sound red wine.

Put the pork rind or the pig's foot at the bottom of the casserole and on top of it the seasoned beef. Arrange the vegetables all round and pour over the Armagnac. Warm the red wine a little and pour it over the beef. It should just cover the meat. Cover the casserole with greaseproof paper, so that it is completely sealed, and then put on the lid.

Cook it over a slow fire for 1½ hours. In the farmhouses it is then taken off the fire and the casserole put on to the hearth over the hot cinders and left there for 24 hours. In a modern kitchen it can be left all day in the slowest possible oven.

An hour before serving, take it out, leave it to cool a little so that the fat can be taken off the sauce (if it has been cooked with fresh pork rind this is cut up and served with the meat). Heat it up gently.

The *Estouffat* can be made a day in advance, and it will be easier to remove the fat if the dish has cooled overnight. The Armagnac or brandy gives the sauce a wonderful flavour, but half the amount can be used.

ESTOUFFADE DE BŒUF À LA PROVENÇALE

Cut about 3 lb of lean stewing beef into large slices; put them to marinate in the marinade described on p. 93 and leave them for 24 hours.

Take the pieces of meat out of the marinade, and sauté them in bacon fat on both sides. Put the meat into an earthenware terrine, pour over the strained marinade, adding a little more wine if there is insufficient, add fresh herbs, 2 or 3 crushed cloves of garlic, ¼ lb of bacon cut into squares, 3 or 4 carrots, and about ¾ lb of stoned olives, black and green mixed if possible; if the olives are salt, add no salt to the meat. Cover the casserole with a greaseproof paper, then the lid, and cook in a slow oven for

3 hours. Ten minutes before serving skim the fat from the sauce and add 3 or 4 chopped tomatoes.

Serve with ribbon noodles boiled in plenty of salted water, put on to a hot dish with a little olive oil, grated cheese and a ladle of the sauce from the beef. This way of serving *pasta* with a stew or with the *pot-au-feu* is one of the old Niçois dishes, called *Macaronade*.

Red wine instead of white can be used for the marinade.

FILET DE BŒUF EN CROÛTE

Make a pastry crust with 8 oz of flour and 6 oz of pure beef dripping, mixed with a little water.

Have ready a piece of fillet of beef weighing about 1½ lb, seasoned with salt and pepper and larded with a few small pieces of garlic; brown the meat lightly on both sides in butter; take it out of the pan, and in the same butter sauté a few mushrooms, 2–4 oz, cut in slices. Put the mushrooms on the plate with the beef, and to the butter in the pan add a small glass of wine, port or sherry, and let it bubble till it is thick. Roll out the pastry, put the meat on one half of it, the mushrooms and the sauce on the top, cover with the rest of the pastry, making a roll with the ends firmly closed down so that no juice will escape, and bake it on a buttered tin in a moderate oven (Gas 5) for about 25 minutes. Serve it hot with, if possible, a *sauce Madère* (pp. 170–1).

Many modern recipes specify puff or flaky pastry for this dish. I prefer the more homely and old-fashioned dripping crust.

Cold, *bœuf en croûte* makes an admirable picnic dish.

L'ENTRECÔTE AUX HUÎTRES

In the Bordelais and the Basque country they eat fresh oysters accompanied by hot grilled sausages. Édouard de Pomiane gives the recipe in *Le Code de la bonne chère* for oysters to be served at the same time as grilled steak with a highly spiced sauce. Since steak and oysters are the two foods in the world most acceptable to Englishmen and in the form of steak and oyster pudding a time-honoured tradition, this way of combining the two might well be tried.

First of all prepare the sauce by putting into a casserole ½ lb of chopped shallots, covered with a whole pint of wine or Orléans vinegar; let this boil until the vinegar is reduced practically to nothing, and what you have left is in fact almost a purée of shallots.

Now grill the steak, and serve each guest with his helping of meat, a spoonful of the sauce, and a dozen oysters. A mouthful of steak and sauce, then a raw oyster . . . The sensation, says M. de Pomiane, of freshness following the fiery sauce is indescribable.

LANGUE DE BŒUF AUX CHAMPIGNONS

Soak a brined ox tongue for a minimum of 24 hours. Put it in a pan with an onion, a bayleaf, a piece of celery, salt and pepper-corns, cover with water and simmer it until it is tender; it will take 4 or 5 hours. Skin it and slice it.

Prepare a brown *roux* with butter, flour, and a little of the stock from the tongue; stir in a dessertspoon of French mustard, a few mushrooms previously sautéd in butter and 2 or 3 chopped pick-led gherkins; pour this over the strained tongue in a casserole and cook together for 10–15 minutes; a little white wine or cider added to the sauce is an improvement, and cream if you like.

GIGOT DE PORC AUX PISTACHES

For a leg of pork weighing 6–7 lb take about 40 pistachio nuts and 2 cloves of garlic.

Lard the leg of pork with the garlic and the shelled and skinned pistachio nuts.

Roast the pork in the usual way, allowing a good 30 minutes to the pound; put the *gigot* on to the serving dish, drain the fat out of the roasting pan and to the gravy in the pan add a glass of white wine and let this bubble until it has thickened a little. Serve the sauce separately, and a dish of braised celery or baby turnips as an accompaniment.

A leg of pork cooked in this way is also delicious cold, with a potato salad, or a green salad garnished with a few chopped pistachio nuts.

CÔTELETTES DE PORC AU CIDRE

Brown the pork cutlets on each side in very little dripping or pork fat. Take them out, and add to the fat in the pan a table-spoon of flour; let this turn golden, and when it is smooth add a wineglass of dry cider, half as much water, and cook it 2 or 3 minutes.

Put the cutlets back in the sauce, seasoned with salt, ground black pepper, a crushed clove of garlic, and a whole sprig of rosemary, which can be removed later. Cover the pan and put it in a very slow oven (Gas 3) for 30 minutes. Five minutes before serving add a few capers to the sauce.

CONFIT DE PORC

This is made with the fillet of freshly killed pig, not shop meat, prepared and cooked in much the same way as the *Confit d'Oie* (pp. 114–5). When the fillet has been salted 5 or 6 days,* it is cut into convenient-sized pieces, about three inches square, *piquéd* with garlic and seasoned with black pepper.

It is then cooked very gently in pork fat and put into pots, covered with the strained fat, and stored away for the summer. It is essential that the jars of *confit* be stored in a *dry* larder.

* In the English climate 2 days' salting is sufficient.

When it is to be used, the jar is put in a warm place, on top of the stove, until the dripping is sufficiently melted to allow the pieces to be taken out easily. The pork emerges rose-pink (due to the original salting), just sufficiently perfumed with garlic and delicious to eat cold with a potato salad. It can also be used in soups and *Garbures* (pp. 29–30), *Cassoulets*, and in the same way as *Oie en Confit*.

PÂTÉ DE FOIE DE PORC DU PÉRIGORD

When a pig is killed and cut up for ham and bacon an excellent terrine can be made from the liver.

You will need equal quantities of liver and unsmoked bacon. Chop the liver very finely, so that it is reduced to a purée. Mix it with the bacon, also finely chopped, adding salt (taking into consideration the degree of saltiness of the bacon), black pepper, 1 or 2 cloves of garlic, 2 or 3 shallots, and spices such as mace and a pinch of ground cloves. Put the mixture into an earthenware terrine lined with slices of bacon.

Pour in a small glass of brandy, and on the top of the *pâté* put a pig's foot cut in two, 2 carrots sliced, 2 onions, a bouquet of thyme, rosemary and a bayleaf, a glass of white wine and one of water. Put the terrine into another pan containing water, cover it, and cook in the oven for 3 or 4 hours very slowly.

Remove the pig's foot and the vegetables and leave the terrine to cool. There should be a good jelly round the *pâté* from the pig's foot. Seal the *pâté* with a layer of pure pork lard.

PIEDS DE PORC SAINTE MÉNÉHOULD

If the pigs' trotters have been salted they must be soaked in water for at least 12 hours before being cooked. Tie them together, two at a time, in opposite ways, with tape, to prevent them falling apart while cooking. Put them into a deep pan and cover them with boiling water in which you have put a glass of white wine and a very little vinegar, an onion stuck with cloves, 2 small carrots, a leek, a branch of thyme, 2 bayleaves, and 2 or 3 peppercorns. Add salt only if the trotters have not been previously salted.

Let them simmer for 3–4 hours until they are tender. Drain them and leave them to get cold. Untie them, cut each trotter in half lengthways and dip each one in melted pork fat or good dripping, then coat them with fine breadcrumbs. Put them under the grill to brown, turning them over and over until they are evenly done.

A mustard sauce, or a *Sauce Tartare*, can be served with them.

FRENCH RECIPE FOR BOILING A HAM

After having soaked, thoroughly cleansed, and trimmed the ham, put over it a little very sweet clean hay, and tie it up in a thin cloth; place it in a ham kettle or braising pan, or any other vessel as nearly of its size as can be, and cover it with two parts of cold water and one of light white wine (we think the reader will perhaps find *cider* a good substitute for this); add, when it boils and has been skimmed, four or five carrots, two or three onions, a large bunch of savoury herbs, and the smallest bit of garlic. Let the whole simmer gently from 4 to 5 hours, or longer should the ham be very large. When perfectly tender, lift it out, take off the rind, and sprinkle over it some fine crumbs, or some raspings of bread mixed with a little finely minced parsley.

Obs. Foreign cooks generally leave hams, braised joints, and various other prepared meats intended to be served cold, to cool down partially in the liquor in which they are cooked; and this renders them more succulent; but for small frugal families the plan does not altogether answer, because the moisture of the surface (which would evaporate quickly if they were taken out quite hot) prevents their keeping well for any length of time. The same objection exists to serving hams laid upon or closely garnished with savoury jelly (*aspic*) which becomes much more quickly unfit for table than the hams themselves.

These considerations which may appear insignificant to some of our readers, will have weight with those who are compelled to regulate their expense with economy.

Modern Cookery, 1855
by Eliza Acton

BAKED HAM

This way of baking hams is very successful. After the ham is soaked and cleaned, put it into a baking tin in a moderate oven until the ham is warmed through. Then remove the ham, fill the tin with water, and put the ham on a rack or grid standing in the pan.

For a gas or electric oven, cover it with greaseproof paper, and cook it at a medium heat for about 20 minutes to the pound.

If you put cider instead of water into the pan you will have the basis of an excellent sauce.

POULTRY AND GAME

POULTRY

ROAST CHICKEN

I came back to Paris after the long sad years of the Occupation.
I will tell all about that, and I wandered around the streets the
way I do and there in a window were a lot of etchings and there
so pleasantly was one by Dufy, it was an etching of kitchen utensils, in an inspired circle and at the bottom was a lovely roasted
chicken, God bless him, wouldn't he just have a lovely etching by
him in the window of a shop and of lots of kitchen utensils, the
factories could not make them, but he had, and the roast chicken,
how often during those dark days was I homesick for the quays of
Paris and a roast chicken.

Gertrude Stein

To roast your chicken successfully the first requirement is that
the bird be young and well fed. Season the chicken inside and
out with salt, pepper and lemon juice. Inside put a large lump of
butter and a piece of lemon peel. Put a buttered greaseproof
paper round the bird, and lay it on its side in the roasting dish,
with plenty of good butter all round. Good dripping can be
used, but there is nothing like a tender chicken cooked in butter.
The oven must be well and moderately heated (Gas 5 or 6).

After 15 minutes' cooking turn the bird over, and see that the
butter is not getting burnt; the oven should now be turned down
a little. After another 15 minutes take the paper away, turn the
chicken breast upwards, and after copious basting with more
butter, if necessary, leave another 10 to 15 minutes to get golden
brown.

Serve the gravy from the pan, in a small dish and, separately,
more butter, melted and flavoured with lemon juice or fresh
tarragon leaves. The classic garnish of watercress is the best one.

Instead of the lemon peel and the butter, a piece of bread, fried in butter and rubbed with garlic, placed inside the chicken, gives a delicious flavour.

POULET AU GRATIN À LA CRÈME LANDAISE

First prepare the following sauce:

In a tablespoon of goose or pork fat sauté 4 sliced onions, a clove of garlic, parsley and a little ham or bacon, all finely chopped. Add the livers and giblets of 4 chickens and, if possible, a knuckle of veal. (As chicken giblets and livers cannot always be bought separately the stock can be made with veal bones, the giblets and liver of the chicken you are going to cook, and possibly ½ lb of stewing beef.) Pour 1½ pints of water over this mixture, simmer it for 1 hour, and then strain it through a sieve.

Now put the chicken on to cook in some good goose or pork fat, but without letting it brown. Season with salt and herbs (thyme or marjoram), and pour over it a claret glass of brandy or Armagnac, and set it alight.

Now pour the prepared sauce over the chicken and cook it for 45 minutes.

Take the chicken out and cut it into four pieces. To the sauce add a cupful of thick cream, a dessertspoon of French mustard and a few small mushrooms which have been previously cooked for 1 minute in butter, and stir in 2 oz of grated Gruyère cheese. Put the pieces of chicken back in the sauce, sprinkle with more cheese, and put it to brown for 10 minutes at the top of a very hot oven.

POULET AU RIZ

1 good chicken, 2 oz butter, 1 lemon, herbs, a carrot, an onion stuck with a clove, a stick of celery, a sprig of tarragon, a clove of garlic, salt and pepper, rice, the neck and giblets of the chicken.

Put the butter inside the chicken, with salt, pepper, a piece of lemon peel and the tarragon. Rub the outside of the chicken with the juice of the lemon and a little salt. Put it in a deep pan with the onion, carrot and celery, and cover with water.

Cook the chicken over a medium flame, covered. If it is a tender bird it will not take more than 45 minutes to cook. This, however, you can only judge for yourself, so when the chicken feels as if it will be cooked in 20 minutes' time, take out the carrot, onion and celery, and the neck and giblets if you have put them in, and put the rice, 2 oz per person, into the pan with the chicken, and let it cook fairly fast until the rice is done (15–20 minutes).

Take out the chicken, cut it in four pieces, and keep it hot while you strain the rice. Have ready a large heated dish, into which you put the rice, and on top of it place the chicken.

A cup of hot cream, into which you have stirred some chopped tarragon and a very small piece of crushed garlic, poured over the chicken in the dish is an added refinement.

POULET AU RIZ BASQUAIS

1 fine chicken, 1 lb tomatoes, 3 or 4 sweet red peppers, 1 lb coarse pork sausage (the Basques have their own particular sausages, called Loukenkas, *very highly spiced), ½ lb rice, herbs, salt and pepper, garlic, spices, a piece of orange peel, onion, paprika.*

Brown the chicken, whole, in goose or pork fat, with a sliced onion, a branch of thyme, a bayleaf, salt and pepper. When it is golden all over, pour over warm water just to cover it, add the sausage, in one piece, and the orange peel, and simmer with the cover on the pan until it is tender; this will take about 40 minutes if it is a tender roasting chicken, anything up to 3 hours if it is one of those purple boiling fowls, so if you are not sure of the quality of the bird, better start it early – heating up later can hardly hurt it.

In the meantime make a *ragoût* of the tomatoes and peppers by sautéing the peppers cut in strips, in goose dripping, and when they are half cooked add the tomatoes, chopped, and seasoned with salt, pepper, and marjoram or thyme. Let them simmer until they are cooked, but don't reduce them to a pulp; stir in a tablespoon of paprika (in the Basque country they have a condiment called *Piment Basquais*, a coarsely ground red pepper stronger than paprika, the colour of cayenne, but nothing like so fiery).

When the chicken is nearly ready, put the rice into a large pan of boiling salted water; cook it for 12–15 minutes, until it is nearly, but not quite, done; strain it and put it in a fireproof pan in which it can be served; now take the chicken and the sausage out of the liquid in which they have cooked; pour a ladle or two of the stock over the rice, and stir it over a very gentle fire; carve the chicken into suitable pieces, and when the rice has absorbed the stock and is quite tender but not mushy put the chicken on the top, pour all round the tomato and pepper mixture, and garnish it with the sausage cut into squares.

The result should be a melting dish of rice, softer than a *pilaff* or a *paëlla*, and not so compact as a risotto, more in fact resembling the *Poulet au Riz*, but with the characteristic Basque flavouring of sweet pepper, tomato, and spiced sausage.

A stewing pheasant cooked in the same way is quite excellent.

POULET À L'ESTRAGON

1 good tender chicken, 2 oz butter, the yolks of 2 eggs, 1 cup of cream, a bunch of tarragon, salt and pepper, lemon.

Rub the outside of the chicken with lemon juice. Mash the butter with salt and pepper and a tablespoon of chopped tarragon, and put this inside the bird.

Poach the chicken, with water barely to cover, until it is cooked. Leave it to cool in the stock. Take out the chicken and place it whole in a deepish serving dish; strain the stock. Now beat up the yolks of the eggs with the cream and another tablespoon of chopped tarragon. Heat about ½ pint of the stock in a small pan, pour a spoonful or two on to the egg and cream mixture, and then pour all back into the pan, stirring continuously until the sauce thickens, but do not make it too thick, as it will solidify slightly as it cools.

Pour it over the chicken in the dish, and leave to get cold. Before serving arrange a few whole tarragon leaves along the breast of the chicken.

POULET À LA SAINTE MÉNÉHOULD

Have a tender young chicken of about 3 to 3½ lb weight (dressed and drawn) trussed as for roasting. Put the bird in a heavy flame-proof pot with 2 oz butter, a chopped shallot or small onion, a seasoning of salt and freshly milled pepper, a few parsley stalks, a sprig or two of thyme and a bayleaf, a crushed clove of garlic, and, when the bird has taken colour in the warmed butter, pour in a glass (4 to 6 oz) of dry white wine.

Simmer the chicken very slowly, from time to time lifting the lid to spoon the butter and wine over the breast of the bird.

When the chicken is nearly done (45 to 55 minutes) take it from the pot, and using a pastry brush, anoint it all over with the beaten yolks of 2 eggs, then press the bird down into a dish in which you have ready about 2 teacups of fine, pale, oven-dried breadcrumbs. Repeat the egg-and-breadcrumbing process, so that the chicken has good protective coats on breast and wings.

If you have a large enough grill, put the chicken underneath and turn it over and over until it is golden, otherwise put it in a fairly hot oven until it browns, or even into a deep pan on top of the stove, so long as it is accessible enough to be carefully turned without damage to the coating of breadcrumbs.

In the meantime get the sauce ready; this is simply a matter of reducing a little the butter and wine in which the chicken has cooked, so that it has the consistency of a good gravy; add perhaps a little cream and a drop of brandy. Or you can, if you like, serve a *Sauce Tartare* previously prepared.

Another and easier method with this dish is to use small chickens, split in half as for grilling, allowing half per person. This makes the initial cooking much quicker and the final operation with the egg and breadcrumbs much simpler.

COQ AU VIN

This is a very old recipe for *Coq au Vin*, and the blood is not in this case added to the sauce as in later recipes.

You need a plump tender chicken (it doesn't *have* to be a cockerel) weighing about 3 lb when cleaned and trussed. Season the bird inside and out with salt, pepper and lemon juice; into a deep heavy pan put 3 or 4 oz of butter and brown the chicken all over in it; pour over a small glass of brandy and set it alight; when the flames have died down, pour in a whole bottle of good red wine — Mâcon, Beaujolais or Châteauneuf du Pape. Add the giblets of the bird, cover the pan and simmer slowly either on top of the stove or in a low oven for about 1½ hours.

In the meantime, prepare 20 or so little onions, browned in butter and glazed with a little sugar and red wine, and ½ lb of mushrooms, sautéd in butter. A few minutes before the chicken is ready, take out the giblets and add the onions and mushrooms.

Remove the chicken on to a hot dish and carve it for serving.

The sauce should by this time be sufficiently reduced to need no thickening, but if it is not add an ounce of butter worked with ¾ oz of flour, put the pan on to a high flame and let the sauce bubble until it is thick enough. Pour it over the pieces of chicken, and arrange the mushrooms and the onions on the top.

LE POULET À LA CRÈME

This is the recipe given by Madame Brazier, of the Restaurant Brazier, one of the famous restaurants of Lyon, in Austin de Croze's *Les Plats régionaux de France*. In those regions the chickens are plump and tender and cook very quickly. When using an older and less well-fed bird it is always advisable to braise it whole, conserving such flavour as it has, carving it for the table when it is cooked, and pouring the cream sauce over the pieces in the serving dish.

Cut a small chicken in four pieces. Melt a good piece of butter in a thick pan, put in a chopped onion and the pieces of chicken, and cook slowly, so that the chicken does not dry up. When it is nearly done cover the pieces with good thick cream and let it bubble for ten minutes. Take out the pieces of chicken and keep them hot in the serving dish.

Into the sauce in the pan beat the yolks of 2 eggs and a squeeze of lemon juice, and let it thicken. Pour it through a fine sieve on to the chicken.

CANARD AUX NAVETS

At the bottom of a fireproof casserole, of a size to hold the duck comfortably, arrange 3 or 4 slices of bacon, 2 onions cut in rounds, 2 or 3 carrots also in rounds, a bayleaf and a small stick of celery.

Place the trussed and seasoned duck on this bed and braise it gently for 10–15 minutes, then pour a glass of white wine over it and let it reduce, add 2 glasses of brown stock and continue cooking very gently with the lid on. A medium-sized duck will take about 1¼ hours. When the duck is cooked take it out and keep it hot. Put the contents of the pan through a sieve, making a fairly thick brown sauce; skim off the fat as much as possible.

Return the sauce and the duck to the pan, and place all round it 2 or 3 dozen baby turnips which you have prepared while the duck is braising, cooked exactly as for *Navets Glacés* (p. 140).

Let the whole dish get very hot and serve it in the casserole.

DUCK WITH FIGS

Put 16 fresh figs to marinate in a half bottle of Sauternes for 24 hours.

Season the duck with salt and pepper and put a piece of butter and a piece of orange peel inside the bird. In a deep earthenware terrine with a lid put 2 oz of butter, and put the duck in the terrine, breast downwards, and another 1 oz of butter on top of the duck. Let it brown in a fairly hot oven (Gas 6), without the lid, for 15 minutes; now pour the butter off, turn the duck over, and pour in the wine from the figs; let this cook 5 minutes and add about ½ pint of stock made from veal bones, the giblets of the duck, 2 sliced onions, 2 carrots, a clove of garlic crushed, and a branch of thyme or marjoram. Put the cover on the casserole and cook in a slow oven (Gas 3) for 1 hour, until the duck is tender.

Now take out the duck and remove the vegetables and giblets; leave the lid off the casserole, turn the oven up and let the juice bubble for 15 minutes to reduce it; put in the figs, and let them cook 5 minutes if they are the very ripe purple ones, 10 minutes if they are green figs; take them out and arrange them round the duck. Leave the stock to cool. Remove the fat and pour the liquid over the duck and figs; it should set to a light jelly.

Serve the duck with a plain green salad.

CANARD EN DAUBE

You need 1 large duck or 2 small ones. One which is old and too tough for roasting will do very well for this dish.

Prepare a number of little strips of bacon and the following mixture of herbs:

A handful of parsley, 2 shallots, chives, a clove of garlic, a bayleaf, a sprig of thyme, a few leaves of basil, salt, pepper, a scrap of grated nutmeg.

Chop all these very finely and roll each strip of bacon in this mixture. Make incisions all over the duck and lard it with the pieces of bacon. Truss the duck and put it into a casserole or braising pan into which it just fits, and pour over it two tumblers of white wine, the same quantity of water and a liqueur glass of brandy. Cover the pan and cook the duck very slowly indeed for 3–4 hours. The sauce will reduce and, when cold, should turn to jelly.

When the duck is cooked, place it in the serving dish; leave the sauce to get cold, so that you can take off the fat, warm it again slightly and then pour it over the duck, and leave it to set. The duck will be very well cooked, so it will be perfectly easy to carve at the table.

If you are serving baked potatoes and have guests who like garlic, have a dish of *aïoli* (a mayonnaise which has been made with 2 cloves of garlic crushed in the bowl before putting the egg in) and put this on the potatoes instead of butter.

COLD DUCK WITH ORANGE AND CHERRY SAUCE

1 duck, carrots, onions, bacon, white wine, seasoning, herbs, garlic, mushrooms, oranges, maraschino cherries.

First of all prepare a stock by browning a sliced onion and the giblets of the duck in a little bacon fat. Add 2 carrots, seasoning and herbs, and a few bacon rinds. When it is all turning brown pour in a glass of white wine and let it simmer 2 or 3 minutes. Add 1½ pints of water and let the stock cook over a moderate fire for about 40 minutes.

In a braising pan put a little more bacon fat, another onion sliced thinly, 2 more carrots, 2 rashers of bacon, a pinch of mace, salt and pepper, a branch of thyme, 2 oz of mushroom stalks, and a crushed clove of garlic. Let this mixture melt in the fat, then put in the trussed duck, seasoned with salt and pepper, and with a strip of orange peel in its inside.

Let it brown very lightly in the fat, then pour in a glass of white wine. Let this reduce by half, then add 2 tumblers of the prepared stock, strained. Cover the pan and let it simmer for about 1½ to 1¾ hours, until the duck is tender. It must now be left to cool in its sauce.

Next day take out the duck and put it on a long serving dish. Skim all the fat off the sauce, warm the sauce again, then press it through a fine sieve, vegetables included, but not the bacon, which would give it too strong a flavour.

Put the resulting purée into a small pan, and into it stir the

rind of an orange which has been thinly pared, cut into strips
and blanched 5 minutes in boiling water. Add the juice of
the orange, a dozen maraschino cherries and a tablespoon of the
maraschino syrup. Let it all simmer together a minute or two,
then leave it to cool.

The duck can be decorated with a few quarters of orange and
surrounded by some shiny green watercress. The sauce is served
separately. All you need with this duck is perhaps a baked potato,
but even this is not essential. Don't overdo it by having an orange
salad or green peas.

CANARD À L'ALBIGEOISE

In a fireproof casserole large enough to hold the duck put a little
olive oil or butter; in this sauté ¼ lb of bacon cut in pieces, and
20 small onions; put in the duck, trussed as for roasting, and let
it brown all over; sprinkle over a little flour, and when it has
turned golden add 2 glasses of vegetable stock, salt, pepper, a leek
cut in pieces, a stick of celery cut up, a branch of thyme and one of
fennel, a small spoonful of paprika, and a tablespoon of sugar.
Cover the pan and simmer for 1½ hours, until the duck is tender.

Take the duck out of the pan and keep it hot; remove the fat
from the sauce as much as possible and reduce it by letting it boil
fiercely, then press it through a sieve.

In the meantime prepare a large piece of bread fried in butter
or bacon fat, and spread it with either a purée of apples or with
red-currant jelly; the duck is served on the croûton, with the
sauce poured over, and some extra apple purée or red-currant
jelly separately.

SALMIS DE DINDE À LA
BERRICHONNE

First of all prepare a stock with the giblets, neck and feet of the
turkey, browned in butter with an onion, a carrot, a clove of

garlic, thyme, bayleaf and parsley. Sprinkle with a tablespoon of flour and let it turn golden, then add a claret glass of red wine and 2 of water, and leave to simmer for 1 hour.

In the meantime, cut up the turkey, dividing the legs and wings into two pieces each and the breast into four pieces. Season them with salt and pepper. Put 3 oz of butter into a casserole or braising pan, and when it is melted put in the pieces of turkey; let them turn golden on each side, take them out and keep them aside. In the same butter put ¼ lb of bacon cut into small squares and 1 lb of small mushrooms. When these in their turn have browned, take them out, and to the butter and juices in the pan add a claret glass of red wine and let it simmer 2 or 3 minutes, then add the prepared stock, through a strainer.

Put back the pieces of turkey, covered with the bacon and the mushrooms, and add 2 tablespoons of brandy. Cover the pan, and cook very slowly for 1½ hours. Serve garnished with triangles of fried bread.

TURKEY À LA CHEVALIÈRE

An attractive way of presenting what is left of a cold turkey.

First of all, make a stock from some of the turkey bones simmered with an onion, celery, herbs and mushroom stalks, which you turn into a sauce either with yolks of egg, cream or arrow-root.

You will need about 12 oz of the white meat, minced or chopped, and some neat little fillets cut from one thigh and drumstick. Put the mince into a small pan with sufficient of the sauce to bring it to the consistency of jam, warming gently over a low fire. Dip the fillets in the sauce, roll them in breadcrumbs and fry them golden-yellow in very hot fat.

To serve, put the mince inside a circle of buttered rice (p. 73), arranging the fillets on the outside, alternated with rolls of crisply fried bacon, and have the remainder of the sauce, very hot, separately.

LE CONFIT (preserved goose)

The south-western region of France, the Languedoc, the Landes and the Béarn, is country which is largely given over to the raising of pigs and geese; the *foie gras* of the Périgord district is as famous as that of Strasbourg; the food is southern in character but quite distinct from Mediterranean cooking in that pork and goose fat replace oil as the basis of all the meat and vegetable dishes, and of the soups. In the winter, when the pigs and geese are killed, they are made, in every farmhouse, into the famous *confits*, stored in earthenware jars covered with lard and used gradually throughout the year. Great jars of pure pork lard and goose fat are stored at the same time; the use of this good dripping gives a robust and countrified flavour to the cooking of these regions, and makes even a simple piece of fried bread into something entirely characteristic. I am giving the recipe for the *confit d'oie*, as it is done in the Landes district, but it is only really worth doing for those who have their own geese and a dry airy larder in which to store the jars.

OIE EN CONFIT LANDAISE

Cut the goose into quarters. Put it into a terrine and rub the pieces all over with *gros sel*, both skin and cut side, about ¼ lb of salt to a goose. Take all the fat from the inside and melt it down in readiness for cooking the goose. As the geese we get in England are not specially fattened as they are in France, one goose may not yield sufficient fat to cover the pieces while they are cooking. Pure pork lard or beef dripping may be added to make up the amount, but not vegetable fat.

Leave the goose for 5 or 6 days (this is for freshly killed geese; birds bought from a shop are better left only 2–3 days), at the end of which you take it out, wash it, and put it to cook in the fat, so that it is completely covered, and cook it very slowly, with the lid on, for 2–3 hours, until, when you test it with a skewer at the thickest part of the leg, the juice comes out pink. If it comes out red it is not sufficiently cooked.

Drain the pieces of goose, put them into a deep earthenware jar. Let the fat in which they have cooked get cool, and then pour it through a strainer over the goose until it is well covered. Tie up the jar with paper.

Goose preserved like this should keep for several months, on condition that it is kept, as explained above, in a really dry and cool larder. After removing pieces of goose for use, be sure that the rest is well covered again with dripping.

OIE EN CONFIT AUX POMMES DE TERRE

Put the jar containing the *confit* on the top of the stove or in a cool oven so that the dripping melts sufficiently, and then take out as many pieces as you need; in the dripping which still surrounds these pieces sauté them gently until they are hot. In the meantime prepare some potatoes, either as for the *Galette de Pommes de Terre* (p. 137), or as for *Pommes à l'Échirlète* (p. 136), and serve the goose and the potatoes together.

OIE EN CONFIT À LA PURÉE

Prepare the pieces of goose as for *Oie en Confit aux Pommes de Terre*; serve them on a purée of lentils, or of split green peas, or of dried haricot beans, garnished with quarters of hard-boiled eggs and croûtons of bread fried in the goose fat.

OIE À LA POITEVINE

For this dish a young goose weighing 6–7 lb is the most suitable.

Brown the goose all over in dripping or butter. Add 1 lb of sliced onions and 10 cloves of garlic; let them brown lightly. Add 6 tomatoes cut up, seasoning of salt, pepper and herbs, and a bottle of white wine. Cover the casserole and simmer for about 5 hours, until the bird is absolutely tender.

Pour off the sauce, and press the onions, tomatoes, and garlic through a sieve; leave the sauce to cool so that the fat, of which there will be a good deal, can be drained off. If the goose is wrapped in paper and kept in a covered dish in the slowest possible oven it will keep hot without drying up and will not get overcooked.

In the meantime prepare 2 lb of small pickling onions or shallots, put them into a frying-pan with a little oil and let them brown, turning them over from time to time; when they are golden, add a tablespoon of white sugar and a small glass of red wine or port; let this thicken until it is syrupy. To serve the goose, heat it up gently in the sauce to which you have added a small glass of brandy and the browned onions.

This is one of the best ways of cooking goose. Serve with it a dish of Jerusalem artichokes à la Provençale (p. 146), or some chestnuts and bacon (p. 144).

COU D'OIE FARCI

When the *confits* of goose are being prepared, the necks of the geese are stuffed and cooked at the same time.

The skin of the neck is turned inside out like the finger of a glove and the inside removed. Make a stuffing of a few pieces of trimmings of the goose, an equal quantity of bacon, or of fresh pork, herbs, garlic and spices, the whole mixed with 2 or 3 eggs. Stuff the goose's neck with this mixture (not too full), sew up the ends and cook it in the goose dripping with the rest of the goose.

To be eaten cold, cut in slices like a sausage. A stuffed goose neck is also sometimes added to a *Garbure* (pp. 29–30) or to a *Cassoulet* (pp. 76–8), in which case it is served hot.

LAPIN AU GRATIN

Joint the rabbit, conserving the blood in a small bowl. Marinate the pieces of rabbit for 1 or 2 hours in white wine or cider.

Cut 2 or 3 onions into rounds, sauté them in dripping, add the pieces of rabbit and let them brown. Season with salt, black pepper and a generous helping of fresh thyme or marjoram; add the white wine from the marinade, cover the pan, and simmer gently for 1 hour or so, until the rabbit is cooked.

To the blood in the bowl add as many fresh white breadcrumbs as will absorb it, a handful of chopped parsley and a clove of garlic crushed. Stir this mixture into the sauce of the rabbit, and continue stirring 5 minutes over a low flame. Put a few knobs of butter on the top of the pan and brown it very quickly under the grill.

GAME

The following recipes are mainly for country dwellers who are in a position to tire of partridge and pheasant plainly roasted; they can also be applied to birds no longer in their first youth, and to the quick-frozen variety.

PERDRIX À LA PURÉE DE LENTILLES

Clean and truss the partridges in the ordinary way: put them into a pan just large enough to hold them with 3 or 4 oz of butter, a large onion sliced and 2 carrots cut in rounds. When the birds have taken colour pour over them a glass of white wine and let it reduce by half; add seasoning and a glass of good stock, cover the pan, and finish cooking over a very small flame. The exact time depends upon the age of the partridge.

In the meantime, you will have prepared a purée with 1 lb of brown lentils, an onion stuck with 2 cloves, 2 cloves of garlic, 2 carrots and salt. Cover with water, simmer for 2 hours, and when the lentils are quite soft put them through a sieve. In a saucepan mix the purée with half the sauce from the partridges, and work it over the fire until the purée is smooth and of the right consistency.

Serve the partridges on a dish, with the purée all round and the rest of the sauce poured over. Quantities for 6 birds.

PARTRIDGES WITH SOUBISE SAUCE

Prepare the partridges as for roasting. Fill each with a chopped onion previously boiled in milk, seasoned with pepper, salt and rolled in a slice of bacon. Make a stock with the giblets of the birds, a slice of bacon, an onion, a few peppercorns, seasoning and herbs. In this stock simmer your partridges for about 45 minutes.

Now strain the liquor, keeping the partridges hot in the pan, and add it to a previously prepared purée made with 4 large onions simmered in milk until tender and put through a sieve. As well as the stock, add butter and a little cream, so that the purée is thick and rich. Pour it over the birds and garnish with curls of crisp bacon.

PERDRIX AUX CHOUX

Partridges cooked with cabbage is one of the classic recipes of French household and country cooking.

Allow 1 stewing partridge per person and 1 medium-sized cabbage for every 2 partridges; ½ lb of bacon, 4 large carrots, and 8 small smoked sausages for 4 partridges.

Brown the birds in bacon fat; blanch the cabbages in boiling water for 7 or 8 minutes; drain them carefully, cut out the stalks and the hard inner part. Cut the cabbages in fine slices and put a layer at the bottom of a large earthenware pot; on top put the bacon, cut in large slices, the carrots, the sausages and the partridges; season with salt, pepper, a few juniper berries,* 2 or 3 cloves of garlic, 2 lumps of sugar, nutmeg and a little grated lemon peel.

Cover with the rest of the cabbage, moisten with stock, about half-way up the cabbage, cover the casserole, and cook in a very slow oven for 4 or 5 hours.

PARTRIDGE EN PAPILLOTES

For young birds.

Cut a good-sized partridge completely in half, from the neck

* To be bought at Soho shops and large stores such as Selfridges.

to the rump; put some butter into a pan, and sauté the two pieces in it for 8–10 minutes. Take them out, season them with salt, black pepper, herbs, and a little orange or lemon peel; leave them to cool.

Then prepare a piece of greaseproof paper for each half bird, rubbed with butter or oil. Lay a piece of bacon on the paper and the partridges on top. Fold the paper over, with the edges together, and fold down all round to make them air-tight. Put them straight on the grid in a medium oven (Gas 5) and cook for 10–15 minutes.

PERDRIX À LA CATALANE

You don't, of course, use the tenderest little roasting partridges for this dish. More elderly birds, so long as they are nice and plump, will do very well.

Truss your partridges as for roasting and put them into a thick pan, just large enough to hold them, in which you have melted two good tablespoons of pork or bacon fat. Season them with salt and pepper, and brown them all over. Sprinkle them with 2 tablespoons of flour, and stir until the flour and the fat are amalgamated and turning golden.

Now pour over them 2 glasses of white wine – in the Roussillon they use the Rancio wine – an ordinary, not too dry white wine can be used, with a small glass of port added. Add a little water, until the liquid comes a little over half-way to covering the partridges. Cover the pan and simmer over a low fire. Half-way through the cooking add 2 sweet red peppers cut into strips.

In the meantime, peel 24 cloves of garlic (for 4 partridges) and cut a Seville orange into slices, rind included. Throw these into a pint of water, and cook until the water boils. This operation is to remove the bitterness from the orange and the garlic, which are strained and put into a second lot of water and cooked for another 8–10 minutes. The garlic will now taste very mild; anyone who likes their garlic strong can omit this second cooking.

By this time the liquid will be considerably reduced and the whole mixture is added to the partridges, together with the juice of a second orange, and all cooked together another 10–15 minutes, until the partridges are tender.

If the sauce is not thick enough, take the partridges out and keep them hot, turn up the flame and let the sauce bubble until it is sufficiently reduced.

Serve the partridges surrounded with the sauce, the sweet peppers, the orange and the garlic, very hot.

The partridges will take from 2–3 hours to cook, according to how old and tough they are.

The *Galette de Pommes de Terre* (p. 137) is particularly good as an accompaniment to Catalan partridges.

PHEASANT WITH CELERY

Prepare a pheasant in the same way as you would for roasting; braise it with butter, a little stock, some squares of bacon and a glass of port.

Have ready 2 fine heads of celery, cut into thin rounds, blanch them for a few minutes, drain them, and then proceed to braise them, also in butter and stock.

When they are done, stir in a cupful of cream, and add them to the sauce the pheasant has cooked in. If this is too thin, thicken it with the yolk of an egg, and pour it quickly over the pheasant in the serving dish.

ROAST WILD DUCK

Put a tablespoon of salt and an onion into the cavity of the trussed birds, and if they are of the fishy-tasting variety put boiling water to the depth of a quarter of an inch into the baking pan. Bake for 10 minutes, basting the ducks with the water. This removes the fishy taste. Then drain, sprinkle lightly with flour, salt and pepper, baste well with hot lard or butter and roast for

15–20 minutes. Take care not to over-cook them or they will lose their flavour.

A *Sauce Bigarade* (p. 169), or the Orange Sauce on p. 170, is the accepted accompaniment of roast wild duck.

LES PALOMBES À LA BÉARNAISE

The wild doves and the wood-pigeons of the Landes and the Béarn are particularly delicious little birds. The ordinary pigeons which one buys in England are rather dull and dry, but cooked *à la Béarnaise* they can be excellent.

First of all, braise the pigeons in butter, in a covered pan, for 30–40 minutes, until they are tender; take them out, cut them in halves and put into a bowl with the juice of a lemon, a glass of white wine or brandy, salt and pepper, and leave them in this marinade while you prepare a purée made from the hearts of cooked artichokes, at least 3 for each pigeon; put this purée into an earthenware casserole with a lump of butter; sauté the livers of the pigeons in the butter in which the birds have originally cooked, adding the wine or brandy marinade, and press them through a sieve, with the liquid, into the artichoke purée; put the pigeons on top of the purée and heat it gently.

Failing artichokes, a purée of broad beans or of Jerusalem artichokes or of celery will serve quite well.

PLUVIER AUX OLIVES

Put a few stoned green olives, or green olives stuffed with pimentos, into each plover. Wrap them in bacon and roast them in butter.

Serve them on slices of bread fried in the butter in which the birds have cooked and impregnated with the juice which has come out of them during the cooking.

BÉCASSE EN COCOTTE

This way of cooking woodcock differs from the traditional method in that the entrails, which have a very powerful flavour not appreciated by everybody, are first removed from the little birds.

Clean the woodcock, reserving the insides; wrap each bird in a rasher of bacon and place them in an earthenware terrine with a tablespoon of butter or dripping for each one; cover with a buttered paper and the lid of the terrine. Put them into a hot oven and cook them for 20 minutes.

In the meantime fry a slice of bread for each woodcock, and spread them with the entrails of the bird chopped and seasoned with salt, pepper, a pinch of nutmeg, a nut of butter and a scrap of fresh thyme or marjoram. Let these heat 2 or 3 minutes in the oven.

When the woodcock are cooked, put the croûtons underneath them and serve in the terrine. The dripping at the bottom of the terrine will have a most exquisite flavour.

HARE

To make a roast saddle and a terrine from one hare. Hare is cheap, but a whole animal is usually rather large for a small household, and this is a way of combining two delicious dishes without waste and without getting tired of it, for the terrine can be stored for two or three weeks if necessary.

First of all, have the hare cut so that the back is in one piece, and reserve this for the roast.

For the terrine put the rest of the hare in joints into a casserole with a half bottle of red wine, 2 onions cut up, 2 or 3 cloves of garlic, a bayleaf, a tablespoon of marjoram or thyme, and 2 lb of fat bacon, cut in squares. The bacon serves to lubricate the meat of the hare which is very dry, and also to improve the taste which is very strong by itself. *Add no salt.*

Cover the casserole and cook in a slow oven for about 45 minutes; when the meat has cooled take it all off the bones and, with the bacon, put it through the mincer. Season it highly with more marjoram or thyme, crushed garlic, ground black pepper, salt if necessary, a small piece of chopped lemon or orange peel, and powdered mace.

Put a layer of fat bacon rashers at the bottom of a 2-pint terrine (or two smaller ones) and put in your hare mixture, but don't press it down too much. Put more rashers of bacon on the top and moisten with about half the original cooking liquor of the hare (the other half is kept for the saddle).

Now put a piece of greaseproof paper over the terrine, cover with the lid and stand in another pan of water and cook in a low oven (Gas 3) for 1–2 hours, according to the size of the terrines you have used.

When the terrines are cooked leave them to cool. Cover with melted lard or clarified butter, and when cool seal with tin-foil or greaseproof paper, and store in a cool larder, or the refrigerator.

The terrine can be eaten either with hot toast as a first course, or as a main course with baked potatoes served on separate plates and a salad such as Orange and Celery, Orange and Endive, Fennel or Cucumber (see chapter on Salads). The recipe for this terrine as it appeared in the original edition of this book contained an addition of aspic jelly, but it is simpler to make in the present version. Also, I have come to the conclusion that it keeps better without the jelly.

Roast Saddle of Hare. Prepare the saddle for cooking by seasoning with ground black pepper, and wrapping first in rashers of bacon and then in a piece of greaseproof paper, and put it in a self-basting pan with plenty of good beef dripping.

Put it into a hot oven (Gas 7 or 8) and roast for 20 minutes.

In the meantime, take the strained liquor in which the pieces of hare for the terrine were cooked, put it in a shallow pan and simmer it until it is reduced and thick. (If it has been salted, the reducing process will make it too salt.)

Take the saddle out of the oven, carve it in thin long pieces and put these into the sauce. Strain the fat out of the pan, and to the remaining juices add a little port or red wine and a little water. Cook this a minute or two and add it to the sauce and the pieces of hare. Cover the pan and cook in a slow oven for about 15 minutes until the hare looks quite done.

As an accompaniment serve a purée of chestnuts (p. 144) and red-currant jelly.

RÂBLE DE LIÈVRE BOURGUIGNON

As in the previous two recipes, the saddle will serve three or four people, the rest of the hare in this case being used for a *civet* or a Jugged Hare.

Put plenty of good dripping or butter over the saddle, cover with a buttered paper and roast for about 40 minutes in a medium to fast oven. When it is done, put in the serving dish to keep hot, pour off the fat, and to the juices in the pan add a cup of cream and half a cup of fine smooth chestnut purée (p. 144).

Pour over the saddle, and serve red-currant jelly as well.

This is really a first-class dish.

AILLADE DE LEVRAUT

1 young hare, ½ lb fat bacon, 2 oz garlic, 2 oz shallots, the liver and blood of the hare, half a tumbler of red-wine vinegar.

Chop finely the bacon, the shallots, the garlic and the liver of the hare. Add the red-wine vinegar, the blood of the hare, and seasoning of salt, black pepper, mace and a little thyme or marjoram. Put this mixture into a small oval copper or earthenware pan and let it simmer very gently for 2 hours. Care must be taken that it does not stick to the bottom of the casserole; should the *aillade* dry up, add a little warmed red wine or vinegar, so that the mixture remains smooth and liquid.

When the *aillade* has been cooking for 1 hour, put the hare on to roast (if the hare is not a young one, the saddle only can be used) with plenty of dripping and covered with a greaseproof paper. It will take about 1 hour to cook if it is whole; 40 minutes for a saddle. When it is ready, put the *aillade* on the serving dish and the hare on top.

A sauce can be made from the juices in the pan, with the addition of red wine or port and a little water.

CIVET DE LIÈVRE LANDAIS

Have the hare cut into the usual pieces. Brown them slightly in goose or pork fat. In an earthenware casserole brown 12 shallots chopped fine, 2 or 3 cloves of garlic, and ¼ lb of bacon or gammon cut in dice (in the Landes they use *Jambon de Bayonne*). Add a glass of red wine, let it reduce a little, add 2 glasses of stock or water and a tablespoon of thick tomato purée (or 6 ripe tomatoes previously grilled and skinned) and an ounce of dried cèpes. Put in the pieces of hare, cover the casserole and cook very slowly for 2–3 hours, until the hare is quite tender.

The sauce should by this time be sufficiently reduced to need no further thickening, but if it is too thin, pour it off into a wide pan, keeping the hare hot in the casserole, and reduce it very quickly for a few minutes.

LES FILETS DE LIÈVRE À LA PROVENÇALE

Cut fillets from the back of the hare in long, fairly thick slices; *piquez* each fillet with a small piece of bacon, season with salt and pepper and sauté them gently in oil or bacon fat, turning them over several times and adding more fat, if necessary. They will take 20 to 30 minutes to cook, as they must be well done.

10 minutes before serving add a wineglass of red or white wine to the pan, 2 tablespoons of thick tomato purée, and a little finely chopped garlic. Continue simmering, with the cover on the pan, and serve garnished with croûtons of fried bread.

VEGETABLES

VEGETABLES

GARLIC

Anyone who may be alarmed by the quantities of garlic used in some of the recipes in this book, particularly in the Catalan and Provençal dishes, may be interested in the following story of the beautiful mannequin who found out how to indulge her insatiable appetite for garlic and at the same time keep her job. That girl was perfectly right. Eating garlic is a question of habit and digestion. There is also the indisputable fact that garlic changes its character according to the amount used. Half a clove crushed into the salad dressing has a more penetrating aroma than a ½ lb stewed with a chicken.

As a matter of fact, the best way of cooking that *Poulet Béarnais* of which Ford Madox Ford writes, is to place the peeled cloves of garlic (by all means use 2 lb if you can face peeling so much) *underneath* the chicken before putting it on to roast. The perfume coming from the kitchen while the roasting is going on is indescribably delicious. The chicken (or, for that matter, a leg of mutton) will be permeated with the flavour, but not unduly so; those who enjoy it may eat the garlic, impregnated with the juice from the roast, while those who do not can do without.

I came yesterday, also in Fitzroy Street, at a party, upon a young lady who was the type of young lady I did not think one ever could meet. She was one of those ravishing and, like the syrens of the Mediterranean and Ulysses, fabulous beings who display new creations to the sound of harps, shawms and tea-cups. What made it all the more astounding was that she was introduced to me as being one of the best cooks in London — a real *cordon bleu*, and then some. She was, as you might expect, divinely tall and appeared to appear through such mists as surrounded Venus saving a warrior.

But I found that she really could talk, if awfully, and at last she told me something that I did not know — about garlic . . .

As do — as *must* — all good cooks, she used quantities of that bulb. It occurred to me at once that this was London and her work was social. Garlic is all very well on the bridge between Beaucaire and Tarascon or in the arena at Nîmes amongst sixteen thousand civilized beings . . . But in an *atelier de couture* in the neighbourhood of Hanover Square! . . . The lady answered mysteriously: No: there is no objection if only you take enough and train your organs to the assimilation. The perfume of *allium officinale* attends only on those timorous creatures who have not the courage as it were to wallow in that vegetable. I used to know a London literary lady who had that amount of civilization so that when she ate abroad she carried with her, in a hermetically sealed silver container, a single clove of the principal ingredient of *aïoli*. With this she would rub her plate, her knife, her fork and the bread beside her place at the table. This, she claimed, satisfied her yearnings. But it did not enchant her friends or her neighbours at table.

My instructress said that that served her right. She herself, at the outset of her professional career, had had the cowardice to adopt exactly that stratagem that, amongst those in London who have seen the light, is not uncommon. But when she went to her studio the outcry amongst her comrades, attendants, employers, clients and the very conductor of the bus that took her to Oxford Circus had been something dreadful to hear. Not St Plothinus nor any martyr of Lyons had been so miscalled by those vulgarians.

So she had determined to resign her post and had gone home and cooked for herself a *Poulet Béarnais*, the main garniture of which is a kilo — 2 lb — of garlic per chicken, you eating the stewed cloves as if they were *haricots blancs*. It had been a Friday before a Bank Holiday, so that the mannequins at that fashionable place would not be required for a whole week.

Gloomily, but with what rapture internally, she had for that space of time lived on hardly anything else but the usually eschewed bulb. Then she set out gloomily towards the place that she so beautified but that she must leave for ever. Whilst she had been buttoning her gloves she had kissed an old aunt whose protests had usually been as clamant as those of her studio-mates. The old lady had merely complimented her on her looks. At the studio there had been no outcry, and there too she had been congratulated on the improvement, if possible, of her skin, her hair, her carriage . . .

She had solved the great problem; she had schooled her organs to assimilate, not to protest against, the sacred herb . . .

Provence
by Ford Madox Ford (pub. George Allen & Unwin, 1938)

HERBS

People who seriously intend to have good cooking grow as many kitchen herbs as they can, so as to have them always fresh. Nowadays, supermarkets and enterprising greengrocers carry a wide range of fresh herbs; and Middle Eastern and oriental shops are good places to look for uncommon ones. Most garden centres sell the basic herbs, and the following specialist nurseries can provide virtually any herb you may want: Arne Herbs, Limeburn Hill, Chew Magna, Avon, BS18 8QW; Cheshire Herbs, Fourfields, Forest Road, near Tarporley, Cheshire, CW6 9ES; Iden Croft Herbs, Frittenden Road, Staplehurst, Kent, TN12 0DH; Poyntzfield Herb Nursery, Black Isle, by Dingwall, Ross & Cromarty IV7 8LX.

For seeds and plants of kitchen herbs, write for growers' catalogues. When ordering tarragon plants, be very firm about them being the *True French* variety, or you may be fobbed off with a plant which, although it grows easily, has no flavour whatever.

Dried herbs should be bought in very small quantities, and stored in air-tight jars as they quickly lose their flavour.

THE POTATO

In 1749 the Paris *Journal* declared of the potato '*voilà le plus mauvais de tous les légumes dans l'opinion générale*'. In our own day we have witnessed the enraged British housewife, backed up by an indignant press, deprived of her national birthright, obliged to queue for a pound or two of potatoes. Too well we know to what base uses those potatoes were put. Boiled to ruins on the outside, and hard within, battered to a grey pulp by a blunt instrument, interspersed with lumps like a boarding-house mattress. Well might the French press repeat its criticism of two hundred years ago.

Yet the potato can be a lovable vegetable. Its uses are wide; it can, if well treated, accompany almost any dish with distinction; makes a most admirable soup, and, richly cooked with cheese or simply baked in its jacket and eaten with butter and freshly ground salt, is a dish fit for any *gourmet*.

THE COOKING OF POTATOES

For *sauté potatoes* cook the potatoes in their skins; peel, slice and sauté them gently in dripping or butter, adding a little chopped onion and parsley at the end.

Potatoes for salad should also be cooked in their skins, peeled and mixed with the dressing or mayonnaise while still warm.

For *Pommes Pailles, Allumettes* and all variations of chips, the raw potatoes should be plunged into plenty of water to wash away the outer starch which otherwise makes them stick together in the cooking. Drain and dry them thoroughly before cooking.

Put *new potatoes* into boiling water.

Go to the extra trouble of *mashing* potatoes through a sieve and adding *warmed* milk.

To keep *boiled* potatoes hot cover them with a clean tea-cloth instead of the lid of the serving dish. This absorbs the moisture and results in dry and floury, instead of sodden, potatoes.

Mashed fried potatoes should be done in bacon fat, very little of it, and watched constantly.

Rub the outside of potatoes for *baking* with a coating of salt.

Baked potatoes are delicious eaten with *aïoli* instead of butter.

GRATIN DAUPHINOIS
(Escoffier's recipe)

Peel and slice thinly and evenly 2 lb of raw waxy potatoes.* Put
them in a basin and add salt, pepper, grated nutmeg, a beaten
egg, a pint of scalded milk, and ¼ lb of grated Gruyère cheese.
Mix all well together. Put them into an earthenware dish, rubbed
with garlic, and well buttered, spread the surface with a generous
coating of grated cheese, add several nuts of butter, and cook in
a medium oven for 40–45 minutes.

Gratin Savoyard is made in the same way, the milk being replaced
by *consommé*. But there are those who claim that only the *Savoyard*
dish should be made with cheese and that the *Dauphinois gratin*
should contain potatoes and cream only (I agree with this view).
In that case the amount of cream is half a pint to a pound of
potatoes.

POTATOES EN PAPILLOTES

Nicolas Soyer, grandson of the famous Alexis, spent years per-
fecting the system of paper-bag cookery and in 1911 published a
book extolling its advantages. Indeed they are many. I can vouch
for the excellence of this method for new potatoes.

Scrape 24 very small new potatoes. Put them on a fair-sized
piece of greaseproof paper, with 2 leaves of mint, a little salt and
2 oz of butter. Fold the paper over and then fold down the two
edges so that the bag is completely sealed. Put it into a preheated
oven, on to the grid (Gas 5), and cook for about 35 minutes.
They will come out perfectly cooked, buttery and full of flavour.
Larger potatoes can be cut in half.

---

* Failing a true waxy variety the best alternative is to use large new King Edwards.

POMMES FONDANTES

This is the most delicious way of cooking new potatoes. Have them well scraped, washed and dried. Choose a thick pan, either a small frying-pan or saucepan or sauté pan of a size which will accommodate the number of potatoes you are going to cook so that each one lies on the bottom of the pan with very little room to spare, or the butter will be wasted and may burn. For 1 lb of potatoes (as much the same size as possible) you need about 1½ oz of butter. Melt it very gently in the pan, put the potatoes in whole. Cover the pan and cook over a low flame. After 10 minutes have a look at them, and when they are getting brown turn them over very carefully and cover the pan again. Small potatoes will take 20–25 minutes, larger ones 10 minutes longer. They should be golden on the outside (but not hard like roast potatoes) and melting inside. Margarine simply will not do for this kind of cooking; it leaves a sediment at the bottom of the pan, which sticks and burns; in any case the flavour of the butter is essential to the dish.

POMMES DE TERRE À L'ÉCHIRLÈTE

This is a way of cooking potatoes from the Périgord district, first class with grilled steak or roast game or by themselves.

Cook whole fairly small potatoes, in just enough water or, better still, stock, to cover them, adding 2 cloves of garlic; cover the pan. By the time the liquid is absorbed they should be cooked. Now put them in a pan with a tablespoon of goose or pork fat and the garlic and cook them slowly until they are brown all over. Turn them over two or three times.

Large potatoes cut in halves or quarters can also be success-fully cooked by this excellent method.

POMMES DE TERRE AU GRAIN DE SEL, SAUCE BOUILLADE

Peel and cut into inch squares 1 lb of waxy potatoes. Throw them into boiling water salted with *gros sel*; when they are cooked, strain them, return them to the pan and dry them over a low flame, shaking the pan.

Serve them with the *All Grenat* or *Sauce Bouillade* (p. 171–2) poured over.

GALETTE DE POMMES DE TERRE

Peel about 1½ lb of potatoes and slice them very thinly and evenly. Wash them in plenty of cold water. In a thick frying-pan heat a tablespoon of butter and one of oil (the mixture of butter and oil gives a good flavour, and the oil prevents the butter from burning).

Put the potatoes into the pan and spread them evenly; season with nutmeg, salt and ground black pepper; turn the heat down as soon as they start to cook, cover the pan and leave them cooking gently for 15 minutes; by this time the under surface will be browned and the potatoes coagulated in such a way as to form a pancake; turn the *galette* over and leave the other side to brown for 3 or 4 minutes; serve either turned out whole on to a flat dish or cut into quarters.

LES ÉPINARDS DU CHANOINE CHÉVRIER

This recipe was given by Jeanne Savarin in August 1905 in *La Cuisine des familles*, a weekly magazine of the nineteen hundreds, published in Paris and sold for five centimes a copy.

The Abbé Chévrier, contemporary of my great-great-uncle, left a reputation in Bresse for being the perfect gourmet; he and

Brillat-Savarin were the best friends in the world; the Abbé, however, did not always disclose his culinary secrets to Brillat-Savarin.

Amongst other delectable things, Brillat-Savarin was excessively intrigued by the spinach cooked in butter of the Abbé Chévrier. 'Nowhere,' he used to say, 'does one eat spinach, simple spinach cooked in butter, to compare with his. What can be the secret?' Brillat-Savarin's mind was finally put at rest; he discovered the famous secret. Here it is.

On Wednesday (for Sunday) choose your spinach, young leaves, neither too old nor in flower, of a good green and with their middle ribs. In the afternoon clean the spinach, removing the stalks, and wash it carefully. When it is tender, drain it in an enamel or china colander; drain out as much water as possible by pressing the leaves firmly down in the sieve; then chop them finely.

Now put them in a pan (enamel or glazed earthenware) with some fine fresh butter and put on to a very low fire. For a pound of spinach allow ¼ lb of butter. Let them cook gently for 30 minutes, then take them off the fire and let them cool in the same pan. They are not to be served today.

Thursday: Add another 1½ oz of butter to the spinach, and cook again for 10–15 minutes over a very low fire; again leave them to get cold; they are not to be served yet.

Friday: Exactly the same operation as the previous day; the same quantity of butter, the same length of cooking. Do not be tempted.

Saturday: Again the same operation as Thursday and Friday. Beware of temptation; the spinach will be giving out a wonderful aroma.

Sunday: At last the day for your expected guests has arrived.

A quarter of an hour before you intend serving the dinner, put the spinach again over a low flame, with two good ounces of butter, for 10–12 minutes. This time, take them out of their pan and put them in a warmed vegetable dish and serve them very hot.

In the course of five daily cookings, your pound of spinach has absorbed 10½ oz of butter. Such was the Abbé Chévrier's secret.

As well as the 10½ oz of butter the spinach has absorbed, it has also reduced to practically nothing. It is certain that the butter does give the spinach a most delicate flavour, but it is advisable to cook at least 2 or 3 lb if all this performance is to be gone through. The recipe is not one to be taken too seriously.

ENDIVES AU BEURRE

These are the Belgian endives or chicory as they are sometimes called in England – the long smooth ones.

Do not cut or wash the endives, or they may turn bitter. Take off the outside leaves and wipe the endives with a clean cloth. Put them into an earthenware or glass casserole, with 2 or 3 fair-sized pieces of butter, and cook them covered over a moderate flame, or in the oven.

Towards the end of the cooking the butter should be all used up and the endives tender and golden brown. At this stage add a little salt and a squeeze of lemon juice.

One of the best vegetables there is to eat as a separate course.

BRAISED CELERY

Clean 2 or 3 heads of celery and cut each one in half lengthways. Blanch them in boiling water for 10 minutes. Drain them carefully, put them into a fireproof dish with 1 or 2 oz of butter, cover the pan and cook slowly until they are tender. 5 minutes before serving add, if possible, 2 tablespoons of meat glaze, which makes all the difference to this dish.

TURNIPS

It seems a pity that childhood prejudices should have almost banned turnips from our tables. Small young turnips are the most delicious of vegetables, and presumably there *are* people who appreciate them in England, for during their brief youth they cost nearly as much as a hot-house peach.

An excellent soup is made from a purée of turnips, and small dice of cooked turnips are an indispensable ingredient of Russian salad, to counteract the sweetness of carrots and green peas. In Greece baby turnips are cut into quarters and eaten raw, with salt, as a *Mézé*; but for this they must be fresh from the garden. The Egyptian Arabs make a pickle of turnips, done in vinegar and beetroot juice to make them pink.

Duck cooked with turnips is one of the classic dishes of the French Cuisine Bourgeoise. Perhaps the best way of all is glazed turnips, either as a separate vegetable or to accompany a steak, or roast beef, or pork.

NAVETS GLACÉS

Put small, whole, peeled turnips (as nearly as possible the same size) into boiling salted water and cook them for 10–15 minutes, until they are nearly ready. Drain them, put them into a small buttered dish which will bear the heat of the flame, sprinkle them with caster sugar, put more butter on the top and 2 or 3 tablespoons of the water in which they have cooked, and put the dish on a very low fire until the sauce turns brown and slightly sticky. Watch carefully to see that it doesn't burn. Spoon a little of the glaze over each turnip and serve as they are, in the same dish.

MUSHROOMS IN CREAM

My sisters and I had a Nanny who used to make these for us over the nursery fire, with mushrooms which we had gathered ourselves in the early morning. I don't suppose they will ever taste quite the same, for the sensations of childhood food elude us in later years — but as a recompense nothing will surely ever taste so hateful as nursery tapioca, or the appalling boiled cod of schooldays.

In the days when cream was plentiful (and nothing but fresh, thick cream will do), I experimented often with this mushroom dish, and the best way of doing it is this:

For four people you must have I lb of mushrooms, and they must be medium-sized, white, button mushrooms, perfectly fresh from the fields. Do not wash or peel them, but carefully rub each one with a clean cloth, and take off the stalks. Put about a teacup of water into a pan and bring it to the boil; add a teaspoon of salt. Put the mushrooms in and cook them for 3 or 4 minutes.

In the meantime, heat your cream, 8 to 10 oz (10 oz is ½ pint) in a small pan, and as it cooks it will reduce and get thicker. Now strain the water off the mushrooms, put the mushrooms back in their pan, and pour the hot cream over them. Cook for 2 or 3 more minutes and serve immediately, extremely hot, on hot plates, in solitary splendour. To have anything else with them would be absurd, but see that there is a pepper-mill on the table, as you cannot add pepper while they are cooking for fear of spoiling the look of the dish.

GRILLED MUSHROOMS

For grilling, the large flat mushrooms are best. Wash them, remove the stalks, and put them on a dish sprinkled with a little salt. This brings out the flavour. Put them into a flat, buttered dish, stalk side up, with a small piece of butter in the centre of each mushroom and grill them gently for about 10 minutes, basting now and again with the butter and adding more if they are beginning to look dry.

Mushrooms, especially field mushrooms, are at their best cooked this way, either alone, with grilled bacon, with steak, or with roast pork.

CHAMPIGNONS CÉVENOLS

Clean I lb of medium-sized mushrooms by wiping them with a clean cloth; put aside the stalks. In a thick pan warm some olive oil, enough to allow the mushrooms to cook comfortably without actually frying. The mushrooms should be put in when the oil is warm, not smoking, and cooked gently for 10 minutes.

Remove them with a draining spoon on to a dish, then in the same oil sauté the stalks cut into small pieces; spread these over the mushrooms, adding a sprinkle of finely chopped garlic and parsley. Still into the same oil throw a handful of fresh white breadcrumbs, and when these are golden, pour oil and bread-crumbs over the mushrooms.

Serve the dish cold the following day; if carefully cooked, without the oil having been overheated, they will be excellent.

TRUFFLES

Most French gastronomic writers make a great to-do about truf-fles; and they are indeed a most remarkable fungus, imparting their delicate flavour to terrines of *foie gras*, stuffed capons and turkeys, fillets of beef, omelettes, and fine sauces; towards the end of the nineteenth century and until 1914, however, their use in what was regarded as *Haute Cuisine* became ridiculously exces-sive, and no dish was considered really refined without a garnish of sliced truffle; more often than not this garnish consisted of parsimonious slices of inferior truffles (there are several var-ieties, and not all of them have the fine flavour of *truffes du Périgord*) added after the dish was cooked and having scarcely any taste at all. The fact is that the most valuable property of the truffle is its capacity to flavour with its perfume any dish in which it is cooked for some time; the truffle itself then loses the greater part of its virtue, having given it to the sauce; it follows that the cutting up of an already cooked truffle, particularly a tinned one, which is the only way we ever get them in England, to decorate a dish, is an expensive and fairly pointless pastime.

Fresh truffles, cooked by themselves, in a sealed terrine with Madeira or champagne, or in a closed crust in the ashes of a wood fire are very delicious, but none of their flavour must be allowed to escape during the cooking. The recipe for cooking them in bacon will be of academic interest only to English readers, except perhaps for a few, fortunate enough to be able to bring them back from France. It is said that one of the most exquisite ways of enjoying their flavour is to leave fresh truffles overnight in a basket of new-laid eggs; next day the eggs, when eaten lightly boiled, will be found to have absorbed the aroma of the truffles.

LES TRUFFES AU LARD

This recipe is best carried out over a wood fire. The truffles are peeled, salted, and each one is wrapped up in a rasher of bacon which is also lightly salted. Wrap each truffle up in an oiled paper, then in another and yet another. In front of the fire arrange a heap of embers, and on this put the little packets of truffles and cover them with more embers, and a few small branches on the top. Leave them to cook for about half an hour.

Remove the paper and put the truffles on a dish with their bacon. They will give off an exquisite aroma, perfuming the air of the dining-room and leading the guests into the sin of greed. Tasting them, it is hard to decide which is the better, the bacon, which has absorbed the flavour of the truffle, or the truffle impregnated with the fat of the bacon . . .

They may be cooked in the oven in the same way, but they will not be quite so good.

La France gastronomique

AUBERGINES EN GIGOT

A recipe from the Catalan coast of France, and perhaps the best way of eating aubergines.

In each whole, unpeeled aubergine, make two rows of small incisions; into these put alternatively small pieces of bacon and cloves of garlic which have been rolled in salt, pepper and herbs, either marjoram or basil.

Put the aubergines in a roasting dish with a little oil poured over them, cover the dish and roast them in a slow oven for about 1 hour.

To be served as a separate course. They are also very good cold, split open, salted, and with a little fresh oil poured over.

LES CHÂTAIGNES AU LARD

Score the chestnuts across on the round side and roast them in a low oven for 15 minutes until both shell and skin can be peeled off. For 2 lb of chestnuts put ¼ lb of bacon cut in pieces into a casserole, add the chestnuts and water to cover. Cook for about 30 minutes.

Serve with turkey, roast hare, or as a separate dish.

PURÉE OF CHESTNUTS

Make a small incision in each chestnut and put them into a tin in a moderate oven for about 20 minutes, when both the skins should peel off fairly easily. Put the peeled chestnuts into an earthenware pot with water to cover and a little pepper, and cook them very slowly either in the oven or on top of the stove for about 1½ hours, until they are soft enough to put through a sieve.

To serve, heat the purée with a lump of butter, a little cream if possible, and a ladle of meat or game stock.

PAILLETTES D'OIGNONS FRITS

Slice large onions into very fine rings. Put them into a bowl containing a little milk, then on to a paper on which you have spread a coating of flour. Fry them in very hot olive oil or dripping. As soon as they are golden and crisp, drain them and serve them with freshly ground *gros sel*.

ROAST ONIONS

Put medium-sized onions, unpeeled, into a roasting-pan. Cook them in a moderate oven, in the same way as baked potatoes, for about 2–2½ hours. The skins then come off, and the onion inside is delicious and full of flavour, to be eaten with salt, pepper and butter.

They are also good cold, as an hors-d'œuvre, with a little oil dressing poured over.

CONCOMBRES À LA CRÈME

Cut peeled cucumbers into fingers and steam them, seasoned with salt, pepper and chopped mint. Prepare a *liaison* of butter and flour with a little milk or cream and stir in the cucumbers when they are cooked.

TOPINAMBOURS EN DAUBE

In a little oil or beef dripping brown a sliced onion, sprinkle in a tablespoon of flour and stir until it is golden; add a small glass of white wine or cider, let it bubble, then put in 1 lb or so of small peeled Jerusalem artichokes, salt, a crushed clove of garlic, a scraping of nutmeg, black pepper, and water just to cover. Simmer until the artichokes are cooked, taking care they don't turn to purée. Before serving stir in a good tablespoon of chopped parsley.

LES TOPINAMBOURS À LA PROVENÇALE

Boil the artichokes in salted water, straining them before they are quite cooked. Cut them in halves and sauté them gently in a little olive oil with 2 or 3 tomatoes cut up, a chopped clove of garlic, and chives and parsley.

HARICOTS À LA GASCONNE

Put 1 lb of haricot beans, of the large variety called butter beans, to soak overnight.

Strain the water off and put them into an earthenware pot with several pieces of fresh pork rind, a little salt and water to cover. Cover the pot and cook them in a slow oven (Gas 3) for about 3 hours, when they should be quite tender.

With a perforated spoon take them out and put them into a heated dish in which you have melted a tablespoon or so of *Beurre de Gascogne* (p. 172), sprinkle a little parsley or chives on the top and serve them either separately, with a stew such as the *Daube Avignonnaise* (p. 91), or with bacon.

LA COURGE AU GRATIN

In slightly salted water cook a piece of pumpkin weighing about 1 lb. Put the pulp through a sieve and then into a pan in which you have melted 1 oz of butter; add ½ cup of milk, a whole egg and the yolk of another; season with salt, pepper and nutmeg; stir in the beaten white of the egg and put the dish in a very hot oven, with small pieces of butter on the top, to brown. Leave it in for 5 minutes only.

SALADS

TOMATES PROVENÇALES EN SALADE

Take the stalks off a large bunch of parsley; pound it with a little salt, in a mortar, with 2 cloves of garlic and a little olive oil.

Cut the tops off good raw tomatoes; with a teaspoon soften the pulp inside, sprinkle with salt, and turn them upside down so that the water drains out. Fill the tomatoes up with the parsley and garlic mixture. Serve them after an hour or two, when the flavour of the garlic and parsley has permeated the salad.

TOMATO SALAD WITH CREAM

Put the required number of whole tomatoes into boiling water to remove the skins. Arrange them in a shallow salad bowl or silver dish.

Pour over them a dressing consisting simply of thick fresh cream into which is stirred a little salt and a tablespoon of chopped tarragon or fresh sweet basil.

A splendid accompaniment for a cold or, for that matter, a hot chicken.

SALADE ARMÉNIENNE

You will need ½ lb of mushrooms, a couple of rashers of bacon, garlic, parsley, pimentos, celery, olive oil and a glass of wine. Slice the mushrooms, sauté them in 2 tablespoons of oil, add a few very fine slivers of garlic, and the bacon cut in squares.

Let this cook a few minutes before pouring in a large glass of red wine; cook fiercely for just 1 minute, then turn the flame low and simmer for 5 more minutes. Stir in a handful of chopped parsley. Leave this preparation to cool.

In the meantime, fill a shallow salad bowl with sliced pimento and celery, dressed with oil and a drop of tarragon vinegar. When the mushroom mixture is cold, pile it on the top. Keep it cool, but don't spoil the flavour by putting it in the icebox.

ICED CUCUMBERS

A pleasant way of serving cucumbers is to have a bowl in front of each place containing salted iced water, a few cubes of ice, slices of peeled cucumbers cut lengthways, and a few cut leaves of mint. This treatment makes the cucumbers deliciously cool and crisp.

CAROTTES MARINÉES

Prepare a marinade of ⅓ pint each of water, wine vinegar, and white wine (or cider), a teaspoon of salt and a teaspoon of sugar, a sprig each of parsley and thyme, and a bayleaf, a small clove of garlic crushed, a pinch of cayenne pepper and 8 tablespoons of olive oil.

Bring the marinade to the boil and throw in 1 lb of young carrots cleaned and cut in halves, or quarters if they are large. Let them boil fairly fast until they are cooked, but not too soft. Drain them, and mix about a dessertspoon of French mustard into the marinade. Pour this over the carrots and leave them to cool.

Serve them cold either as hors-d'œuvre or salad. They can be prepared 2 or 3 days in advance.

BŒUF EN SALADE

To use up a piece of cold spiced beef, or *Bœuf à la Mode*, or beef from an *Estouffat*.

At the bottom of a salad bowl put a layer of sliced tomatoes, seasoning them with salt and pepper, then a layer of small slices of beef, then a layer of cooked potatoes, also seasoned with salt and pepper. Pour over a *Vinaigrette* dressing (oil, tarragon or wine vinegar, French mustard, a little sugar, capers, chopped chives, parsley and lemon peel).

Garnish the salad with quarters of hard-boiled egg.

FENNEL SALAD

The raw fennel roots are washed and cut into small strips, dressed with oil and lemon juice, preferably 2 or 3 hours before serving.

ORANGE AND CELERY SALAD

Inch-long pieces of celery and quarters of orange, with a very little dressing of oil and lemon. Especially good to accompany a terrine of hare or rabbit.

SALADE DE L'ÎLE BARBE

1 lb potatoes cooked in their skins, peeled and cut in slices, 2 cooked red or green sweet peppers in strips, 2 oz ham cut in dice, 1 lobster or crawfish tail cut into rounds, a few rounds of truffle, and a few olives.

Mix all together, seasoned with olive oil, salt, pepper and lemon juice. The truffles can be replaced by a few blanched mushrooms, cut across in thin slices.

A very attractive salad, to be eaten as a separate course.

SALADE JAPONAISE

This fantasy is the recipe given by Alexandre Dumas *fils* in his play *Francillon*. Without taking it too seriously, the combination of mussels and potatoes with white wine and herbs in the dressing produces an excellent salad.

Cook some potatoes in a meat stock, cut them in slices, and while they are still warm season them with salt, pepper, fine olive oil, Orléans vinegar, and, if possible, half a glass of Château Yquem. Chop very finely a large handful of fresh herbs.

In the meantime, cook some large mussels (a third of the quantity of potatoes) in a *court-bouillon* of white wine and water to which you have added a stick of celery; drain the mussels, take them out of their shells and add them to the potatoes. Mix all the ingredients lightly.

When the salad is ready, cover it with a layer of sliced truffles which have been cooked in champagne. The salad must be made 2 hours before serving.

SALAD OF LETTUCE HEARTS WITH MELTED BUTTER

Use only the tenderest of lettuce hearts for this exquisite salad; arrange them in a salad bowl, season them very lightly with salt and a scrape of sugar, and at the last moment pour over them warm melted butter into which you have pounded a very small piece of garlic and a squeeze of lemon juice.

LA SALADE AU CHAPON

A *chapon* is a piece of bread or toast rubbed with garlic, sprinkled with olive oil, and placed at the bottom of the salad bowl. The salad, lettuce, curly endive, or dandelion, is put on the top of the *chapon*, and mixed with the dressing in the usual way. For those who like garlic it is one of the most delicious of salads. Rubbed on bread, garlic retains its full flavour and wonderfully permeates the whole dish.

LES CERNEAUX AU VERJUS

An hors-d'œuvre from Touraine, made with green walnuts.

Cut the walnuts in half and take them out of their green skins. Put them into a bowl and cover them with the juice of white grapes, pressed through a sieve; season with a little pepper and a finely chopped shallot; leave them to marinate at least 1 hour before serving.

SWEETS

SWEETS

GÂTEAU DE MARRONS

Roast about 2½ lb of scored chestnuts for 20 minutes in a slow oven, so that both the shell and skin will peel easily. Finish cooking them in water to cover, strain them and put them through a sieve.

To this purée add about ¼ pint of milk, 2 oz sugar and 1 oz of brandy. Fold in the beaten white of 6 eggs. Prepare a caramel of ¼ lb of sugar with 3 tablespoons of water, and coat the bottom and the sides of a cake tin with it. Pour in the chestnut mixture and cook it in a moderate oven for 1 hour. When it is cold, turn it out and serve it with cream.

GÂTEAU DE MARRONS AU CHOCOLAT

Cook 2½ lb of chestnuts as in the previous recipe and put them through a sieve.

Melt ¼ lb of chocolate in a very little water or black coffee, stir in ¼ lb of butter and ¼ lb of sugar, timing this operation so that the chestnut purée is still warm, and stir the two mixtures together. Pour it into an oiled cake tin, square for preference, and leave it in the refrigerator or in a cold place for 24 hours. Turn it out on to the serving dish.

As this sweet is rather rich, a small amount, with cream separately if possible, is enough for most people. Half quantities work out quite successfully.

MARRONS À LA LYONNAISE

Make a purée from 1 lb of skinned chestnuts (start off with about 1½ lb), cooked in very slightly salted water to which you have added 1 or 2 cloves. Add to the purée 4–6 oz of sugar (according to how sweet you like the chestnuts), 3 oz of butter, 3 yolks of eggs, and finally the whites of the eggs stiffly beaten. A little brandy or rum (added before the whites of eggs) will do no harm.

Pour the mixture into a cake tin and cook for about 40 minutes in a moderate oven. When cold, turn it out, and serve with cream.

This is a very filling sweet, and, although it does not look very large, this amount is ample for eight people.

COFFEE CHESTNUTS

For four people you need about 36 shelled and skinned chestnuts. Put them in a pan with enough water to cover and 2 tablespoons of sugar. Simmer until they are soft.

In another pan (preferably a double saucepan) put the yolks of 2 eggs, a tablespoon of sugar, a teacup of strong black coffee, 2 tablespoons of cream or top of the milk and a liqueur glass of rum. Stir the sauce over a low flame until it thickens and pour it over the strained chestnuts in a silver dish.

LEMON SOUFFLÉ (1)

3 yolks of eggs, 4 whites, 1 lemon (juice and rind), 1½ oz plain flour, 1 breakfast-cup milk, 2 tablespoons caster sugar, 2 oz butter.

Melt the butter, stir in the flour, cook until it is smooth, then add the warmed milk and cook again until you have a smooth white sauce. Add the sugar, the grated rind, the 3 yolks, stir off the fire, then add the lemon juice. When it is cool fold in the beaten whites.

Pour it into a soufflé dish, with a buttered paper band round the top, and cook for about 15 minutes in a hot oven (Gas 6 or 7).

LEMON SOUFFLÉ (2)

4 eggs, 3 tablespoons caster sugar, the juice and rind of one lemon.

Beat the yolks of the eggs with the sugar, the grated rind of the lemon and the juice, for several minutes. Whip the whites and fold them in. Pour into a buttered soufflé dish and cook for 10–12 minutes in a medium-hot oven.

Soufflés made without the addition of flour are very light and creamy, but the whole operation should be performed with speed, and, as already explained on p. 48, the exact heat of the oven and the timing can only be learnt by experience.

OMELETTE SOUFFLÉ AU GRAND MARNIER

For two people you need 3 eggs, 2 tablespoons of sugar, a sherry glass of Grand Marnier, butter.

Separate the eggs; into the yolks stir the sugar and the Grand Marnier, amalgamating them well. Beat the whites very stiffly.

In the meantime, heat a ten- or twelve-inch omelette pan, and have your hot plates and a hot omelette dish in readiness.

Now fold the whites into the yolks, put a small nut of butter in the pan — if the frying-pan is properly heated it will melt instantly. Quickly pour in the egg mixture and give the pan a shake. The outer surface next to the pan will brown at once and the rest puff up. Now take your omelette dish in one hand and the pan in the other, and, holding the pan close to the dish, slide the omelette out, folding it over once as you do so.

An omelette soufflé must be eaten immediately, while it is still frothy and creamy, and as it has only been cooking *one minute* it will soon be cold.

Don't attempt to make more than the quantity given in one pan; for four people double the mixture and make 2 omelettes.

BUTTERED APPLES

One of the nicest and simplest ways of serving apples. Bramleys are best as they turn fluffy when cooked. Put the sliced and peeled apples into a fireproof dish. For 1 lb of apples put 1 oz of butter cut in pieces on the top, 2 tablespoons of brown sugar, and a piece of lemon peel.

Put the dish uncovered, and without any water, into the top of a medium oven, for about 30 minutes. Have a look at them from time to time and turn them over so that all get equally cooked.

They are nice hot or cold, for an open tart or for the filling of an omelette soufflé.

GOUÈRE AUX POMMES

A country sweet from the Berry district of France.

Peel and slice a pound of apples, and put them in a dish with a little sugar and 2 tablespoons of brandy.

Make a batter with ½ lb of flour, 2 eggs, a pinch of salt, 3 tablespoons of sugar and a tumbler of milk.

Stir the apples into the batter and pour it into a shallow buttered tin and cook for 45 minutes in a moderate oven.

APPLES IN CIDER

Peel and slice 2 lb of apples. Put them into a fireproof dish with brown sugar, the amount depending on what apples are being used. Add cider to about a third of the height of the apples.

Cover the dish with a buttered paper and cook for about 30 minutes in a moderate oven; at the end of this time baste the apples with the cider and leave a little longer without the paper, so that the top will get lightly browned. These apples are very good hot or cold.

JACQUES

These pancakes are a speciality of the country districts of Périgord.

¼ lb flour, 1 gill milk, 1 dessertspoon olive oil, a pinch of salt, 1 teaspoon sugar, ½ glass water, 2 eggs, 2 or 3 apples.

Make a pancake batter with the flour, oil, salt, milk, water and eggs; stir it very well, then let it rest for several hours.

Peel the apples and cut them in very thin slices; sprinkle a little caster sugar over them and a squeeze of lemon juice. Heat a small, thick frying-pan and coat with a thin film of oil or butter; drop in a tablespoon of the batter and let it spread out as much as possible; on top of the pancake place 2 slices of apple, cover them with a little more of the batter and turn the pancake over; let it cook a little longer than the ordinary pancake on account of the apples; the pancakes are served flat, sprinkled with sugar, and, of course, as quickly as possible. The apples can be soaked in a little rum or brandy should it be available.

APRICOT COMPÔTE

Apricots are exquisite to eat raw when they are slightly over-ripe, sun warmed and straight off the tree. Otherwise they gain by being cooked, and this *compôte* brings out their slightly smoky, delicious flavour.

Halve the apricots and take out the stones. Cook them gently with water half-way to covering them and about ¼ lb of sugar to 2 lb of apricots. Watch them to see that they do not dissolve into a purée. Take the apricots out of the pan and put them into a dish. Reduce the remaining syrup until it is thick, then pour it over the apricots.

Serve cold. Cream is unnecessary; it would disguise the taste of the apricots.

CHOCOLATE MOUSSE

1 egg per person, 1 oz plain or vanilla chocolate per person.

Melt the chocolate in a thick pan over a low flame with a tablespoon of water. A tablespoon of rum added will do no harm. Stir the chocolate until it is smooth. Separate the eggs and beat the yolks. Stir the melted chocolate into the yolks.

Whip the whites very stiffly and fold them over and over into the chocolate, so that they are perfectly blended, or the chocolate may sink to the bottom. Put the mousse into a soufflé dish so that the mixture just about comes to the top (nothing is sadder than a small amount of mousse hiding at the bottom of a huge glass bowl) and leave it in a cool place to set. Unless in a hurry, don't put it on the ice, as this tends to make it too hard.

Instead of water, the chocolate can be melted in a tablespoon of black coffee.

SAINT ÉMILION AU CHOCOLAT

¼ lb butter, ¼ lb sugar, 1 egg, ½ lb chocolate, 1 teacup milk, 12 to 16 macaroons.

Cream the butter and the sugar until they are well amalgamated. Scald the milk and let it cool, then mix it with the yolk of the egg. Melt the chocolate over the fire, with a very little water, then stir in the milk and egg mixture, then the butter and sugar. Stir this cream carefully until it is absolutely smooth.

In a soufflé dish arrange a layer of macaroons, soaked in a little rum or brandy; over these pour a layer of the chocolate cream, then put another layer of macaroons and so on until the dish is full, finishing with macaroons. Leave the dish in a cold place for at least 12 hours.

HONEY AND HAZELNUT CAKE

This is not really a cake, but a kind of soufflé eaten cold, a Périgordine speciality.

Put ½ lb of honey in a jar in a saucepan of hot water so that it is easy to manipulate. Pour it over 5 or 6 yolks of eggs beaten in a large bowl; add gradually a teacup of sifted flour and a teacup of hazelnuts pounded in a mortar with a little caster sugar; bind the mixture either with a little milk or cream (about ½ cup) or the equivalent amount of butter.

Lastly, add the beaten whites of the eggs, and pour the whole mixture into a buttered cake tin or soufflé dish, and cook it for 40 minutes in a moderate oven. When cold, turn the cake out.

It is also excellent made with walnuts instead of hazelnuts.

CARAMEL RICE

This sweet is inspired by the famous *Crème Brûlée*, one of the loveliest sweets in the world, made with eggs and cream, and burnt sugar on the top. There is no possible substitute for it, but Caramel Rice makes a pleasant, attractive finish to a simple luncheon or dinner.

For four people you need:

1 teacup rice, 1 pint milk, 1 vanilla pod or a large piece of lemon peel, 4 oz cream, 6 oz sugar, the juice of a lemon or an orange, 2 oz candied peel.

Put the milk in the top half of a double saucepan, and put in the rice, 4 tablespoons of sugar and the vanilla pod or the lemon peel. Cover the pan and simmer until the rice is cooked; this takes 1½–2 hours, at the end of which time the rice should have absorbed nearly all the milk and be very creamy without being a cloggy mass. Turn the rice into a soufflé dish, add the lemon or orange juice, and the cream which should be fairly thick, and the finely chopped candied peel. Chill this mixture thoroughly.

Now spread on the top of the rice a layer of sugar about a quarter of an inch thick. Have the grill already hot and put the dish underneath it, fairly close to the heat. In about 2 minutes or even less the sugar will have turned to toffee on the top; the surface should be even and smooth, but with a gas grill this is not very easy. Turn off the grill the second the sugar looks set, as it burns in no time. Serve very cold.

CROÛTES AUX PRUNES

Not exactly a dish for a grand party, but, all the same, an excellent countrified sweet.

For each person cut 1 or 2 slices of new bread, half an inch thick, leaving on the crust. Butter them on one side, and on this side put 5 or 6 raw half plums, stoned, pressing them down and into the bread with a knife; put a little butter and brown sugar into each half plum, and put the slices into a generously buttered fireproof dish, plum side up; put them into a moderate oven (Gas 4) near the top, with a piece of buttered paper over them, and in about 30 minutes the bread will be golden and crisp and the plums cooked with a coating of sugary syrup on the top.

Apricots can be cooked in the same way with good results.

TOURTE DE CITROUILLE

1 lb pumpkin, 2 oz sugar, 1 teacup fresh cream, 20 prunes, 2 oz butter.

Cook the pumpkin in the butter until reduced to a purée. Add the soaked and stoned prunes, the cream and sugar, and keep aside. Make a short crust with ½ lb of flour, ¼ lb of butter, a pinch of salt and a little milk. Leave to rest 2 hours.

Roll out and cut two rounds the size of the pie-dish. Line the tin with one round, put in the pumpkin mixture, cover with the second round of pastry. Cook in a fairly fast oven to start with, turning it down after about 10 minutes.

LA TARTE AU PETIT SUISSE

Make pastry with 6 oz of flour, 4 oz of butter, an egg, 3 tablespoons of sugar and a pinch of salt. Work the pastry as little as possible, and roll it out on a clean floured cloth to fit a 5″ pie tin; the pastry breaks easily, so turn the cloth gently upside down on to the tin, cover the pastry with greaseproof paper, fill with a handful of dry beans and bake it in a moderate oven (Gas 4) for

20 minutes. Remove the beans (keep them in a jar especially for the purpose of baking pastry blind, i.e. without a filling).

In the meantime pound 6 oz of *Petit Suisse* or fresh cream cheese with ½ teacup of cream or milk, 2 yolks of eggs, 4 tablespoons of sugar, a teaspoon of orange-flower water or grated orange peel, and, lastly, the whites of the eggs beaten to a stiff froth. Spread the mixture on the cooked pastry, put it in a moderate oven (Gas 4) for 15–20 minutes.

A beautiful golden crust should form on the top, but look at it from time to time to see that it does not burn.

To be eaten cold.

TOURTEAU FROMAGÉ

Make a pastry with 6 oz of flour, 4 oz of butter, an egg and a pinch of salt. Knead it with a little water and leave it to rest 1 or 2 hours.

Mix together 6 oz of fresh cream cheese (in Poitou, where this recipe comes from, they use goat's cheese; home-made milk cheese or *Petit Gervais* will do), 3 eggs, 4 oz of sugar, 2 tablespoons of cream (or top of the milk), and 2 tablespoons of chopped angelica.

Line a buttered and floured 9″ tart tin with the rolled-out pastry, fill it with the cheese mixture, and bake it in a hot oven (Gas 4) for about 7 minutes and at Gas 5 for 20 minutes.

To be eaten cold.

RASPBERRY AND RED-CURRANT TART

These flat open tarts are made on Sundays and fête days in a great many French households both in the towns and in the country. They are also to be bought in *pâtisseries*, of a better quality than anything we could buy ready-made in England. They are usually baked in a large shallow tin about ten inches across, and served cold. They are not difficult to make and are one of the nicest possible dessert dishes. The point to remember is that fruit which gives out a great deal of juice when cooking should be prepared first, the pastry also baked in advance. When the pastry is cooled it is filled with the fruit and put back in the oven for a few minutes. In this way the pastry does not become sodden with the juice of the fruit.

Make the pastry as described for the *Tarte au Petit Suisse* (pp. 162–3), and bake it in the same way.

Put 1½ lb of raspberries and ½ lb red-currants into a pan with 6 oz of white sugar and let them cook for a few minutes only; the fruit should not lose its shape. When the pastry has cooled, fill it with the fruit, strained, and put it in a moderate oven for 10 minutes.

To the juice of the fruit add a tablespoon of red-currant jelly. Stir this mixture until it is a thick syrup and pour it over the fruit when this has cooled. It will give a fine glaze and a firm consistency. The quantities given will fill an oblong tin ten inches by eight, or a ten-inch round flan tin.

TARTE AUX PÊCHES

This is made in the same way as the *Raspberry and Red-Currant Tart*, the peaches being skinned, sliced and very lightly stewed before being put into the cooked pastry. The syrup can be made in the same way, with the addition of a small glass of peach brandy.

TARTE AUX POMMES

Make a crust as for the *Tourteau Fromagé* (p. 163), spread it on a buttered tart tin and make a few incisions here and there with a fork.

On top of the pastry arrange 2 lb of apples peeled and cut in fine slices, adding about 4 oz of white sugar in between the layers of apple. Bake in a moderate oven for 30 minutes.

The apples should be slightly browned on the surface and

moist inside. A little syrup, made from the peel of the apples, sugar, and a flavouring of either lemon peel, brandy, *calvados*, or sweet cider, can be poured over to form a glaze when the tart has cooled.

TARTE AUX ABRICOTS

This is made in the same way as the Apple Tart above, the apricots being cut in half and stoned but not skinned.

Put a little sugar in each half apricot. Remember that the fruit shrinks considerably in the cooking, and if there seems to be too much to start with it is all to the good.

Stew a few extra apricots with a little sugar and water. Strain off the liquid, reduce it, and use this as a syrup for glazing the tart. If available, a few drops of kirsch or apricot brandy can be added.

LES CRÉMETS D'ANGERS

For every ½ pint (10 ounces) of fresh cream, allow the whites of 2 eggs; whip the cream until it is stiff, then whip the whites of eggs separately. Mix the two together gently. Pour it into little baskets lined with muslin and leave them to drain in a cool place overnight.

Serve them turned out in a bowl, with fresh liquid cream poured over, and a bowl of sugar separately.

SAUCES

Very few of the dishes described in this book need the addition of any elaborate sauce. Meat, chicken or game simmered in wine with vegetables, onions, herbs and garlic need no further adornment. For vegetables, good butter is nearly always the best accompaniment. Chicken and fish *veloutés*, lobster butter and so on, belong rather to the methods of restaurant cooking and professional chefs than to country and household meals; nor are such sauces always an embellishment of the food with which they are served, although nobody would deny that plenty of fresh cream and butter help enormously in the preparation of good food.

Sauce Béarnaise and *Sauce Hollandaise* are classic and delicious accompaniments to grilled meat and fish; I have already described these in some detail in a previous book, so they are not repeated here. As, however, the *Sauce Bordelaise* for fillet of beef, and the *Sauce Bigarade* for roast duck, are both made on a foundation of *Espagnole*, I am giving an easily made version of this sauce, suitable for a small household. These recipes, with meat glaze, the brown and white *roux* given in this chapter, and various sauces explained at the same time as the dishes with which they are to be served (such as the *Beurre Blanc de Vouvray*, or the sauce for roast saddle of hare on pp. 125–6), should give plenty of ideas about the composition of simple sauces to anyone who is at all imaginative about food. Further explanations of the use of wine in sauces will be found in the chapter 'Wine in the Kitchen'.

It will be seen that only a very few of these regional recipes contain flour for the thickening of sauces; whenever possible the consistency should be achieved either by reduction, as explained for the meat glaze (another example is the *Coq au Vin*, p. 108), or with a *liaison* of egg yolks (after adding egg yolks to a sauce it must never be allowed to boil, and cannot be heated up, or it will curdle). Cream should also be thickened by reduction (see *Sole au Vin Blanc*, p. 47).

When a sauce is to be made with a basis of a brown or white *roux*, it must cook for a minimum of 15 minutes, or it will taste of raw flour; and remember that flour should always be sieved before being added to a dish. When flour is used (as in the *Perdrix à la Catalane*) at the beginning of the cooking, the sauce has had plenty of time to absorb the flavours of the bird (or meat) and the wine and seasonings by the time the dish is ready to be eaten. When a sauce such as this seems too thin, don't panic and add a lot more flour at the last minute; let it thicken by fast boiling and reduction.

BROWN AND WHITE ROUX

A *roux* is simply the composition of butter and flour which is the basis of a great many sauces such as *Espagnole*, which is made with a brown *roux*, and *Béchamel*, made with white *roux*.

Melt 2 oz of butter in a small saucepan, and when it barely begins to bubble add 2 oz of sieved flour. Stir carefully over a gentle fire until the mixture amalgamates (2 or 3 minutes in the case of a white *roux*), when it is time to put in the milk or stock or whatever is to be the foundation of the sauce. For the brown *roux* the mixture is cooked about 5 minutes, stirring all the time until it takes on a nut colour; it must not burn, or it will have a bitter flavour. The quantities given will serve to thicken about 1 pint of sauce.

MEAT GLAZE

In the old days meat glaze or *glace de viande* was made with huge quantities of beef and veal and probably 2 chickens as well, the resulting stock being reduced until it was a thick jellied sauce; it was then stored for use. There is no doubt that a small quantity of meat glaze in the larder adds enormously to the joy of good cooking. To make certain sauces, added to the butter in which steaks or cutlets have been cooked, to a simple egg *en cocotte*, to glaze a piece of cold beef, a chicken or duck, for *salmis*, for vegetables such as celery, endive or baby turnips which have been braised in butter, a little meat glaze transmutes ordinary household dishes into the realm of fine cooking.

For a small family it is quite possible to make enough meat glaze to store for a few days without extravagance, and it is worth trying it now and again.

You will need 1–2 lb of stewing steak, shin of veal, or marrow bones, a glass of red wine, 2 or 3 onions, garlic, herbs.

Fry the onions in dripping, then add the beef, in one piece, and brown on each side. Pour over the wine, let it bubble for 2 or 3 minutes and then pour in about 4 pints of water. Add the veal bones, the garlic, and the herbs, but no salt.

Simmer in a covered pan very slowly (this is best done in a low oven) for 6 or 7 hours. Strain the stock into a bowl and leave it to cool. The beef will not be wasted; it will make a good *Bœuf en Salade*, as described on p. 149.

When the fat has solidified, remove it from the stock, which should be jellied. Put the stock in a wide and shallow pan and simmer it until it starts to look syrupy and shiny – something like undiluted Bovril.

It can be stored in little jars with a layer of fat on the top and used as it is needed.

Salt is not added during the cooking, as the reducing process would make it too salty, so it can be added as you use the glaze.

EASILY MADE ESPAGNOLE SAUCE

Make a brown *roux* with 3 tablespoons of butter and 4 of flour; when this has cooked add gradually 2½–3 pints of very good beef stock, made as for the meat glaze already described, but not reduced.

Let this mixture simmer, stirring from time to time, for at least 1 hour, until it is well reduced. You then have a foundation on which to make the *Sauce Bordelaise* and the *Sauce Bigarade*, given in this chapter.

SAUCE BORDELAISE

Reduce a wineglass of white Bordeaux by half, with a pinch of black pepper and a finely chopped shallot.

Stir in ½ pint of *Espagnole Sauce* and let it bubble 5 minutes. Before serving add a tablespoon of chopped parsley.

SAUCE BIGARADE

Bigarade is the French name for bitter or Seville oranges. The sauce is made with a foundation of *Espagnole*.

Reduce ¾ pint of *Espagnole* to about ½ pint. In the meantime cut the peel of 2 Seville oranges into strips and put them into boiling water for 5 minutes. Drain them and add them to the sauce with the strained juice. Heat up gently.

ORANGE SAUCE (a simpler way than the preceding recipe)

When you are going to serve orange sauce with a roast duck or pheasant, have ready the peel of an orange cut into fine strips and blanched 5 minutes in boiling water, and squeeze the juice of the orange.

When the duck is cooked take it out of the roasting-pan and keep it hot on a fireproof dish in the oven. Pour the fat out of the roasting-pan, and to the remaining juices in the pan add a small glass of port, Madeira or Malaga, or a little of the Burgundy you are going to drink with the duck. Let this bubble over a low flame a minute or two while you scrape the juices up and blend them with the wine. Now add a very little water, let it bubble again, and put in the orange peel and juice, and let it cook another minute.

The whole process does not take 5 minutes and can in fact be done while someone else is carving the duck. It is a thin sauce and does not need thickening of any kind.

SAUCE SOUBISE

Cut up 2 lb of onions and cook them in boiling water for 20–30 minutes. Strain them, put them through a sieve, and stir this purée into half its volume of *béchamel* sauce, or thick cream; if to serve with game or poultry, some of the stock in which the bird has cooked is amalgamated into the sauce.

SAUCE MADÈRE

Slice an onion and a carrot finely, and put them in a pan with I oz of butter. Let them melt slowly, then add ½ pint of water and a chopped tomato or a tablespoon of tomato purée, a dessertspoon of meat glaze or a small cube of *Maggi*,* a *bouquet garni* of parsley, thyme and bayleaf, and leave this to cook for 20 minutes.

Now mix 3 teaspoons of flour with a small glass of water and pour it through a strainer into the sauce, stirring all the time. Cook until the sauce thickens and strain into a clean pan. Add a sherry glass of Madeira.

In a small frying-pan melt 2 oz of butter, let it just turn golden, but don't let it burn. Add this to the sauce – it gives a characteristic flavour.

PESTOU

This is the garlic and basil butter added to soups and used as a sauce for *pasta* and for fish in the Nice district in Genoa.

Two medium-sized cloves of garlic, 1½–2 oz of butter, about 6 sprigs of fresh basil, a pinch of salt, 2 tablespoons of Parmesan cheese.

Pound the garlic in a mortar, then add the basil, then the butter and the cheese.

It is also, of course, made with oil instead of butter with the addition of pine nuts, and makes a sauce more like a thick purée.

To serve with *spaghetti* or *lasagne*, this version is better, but for *gnocchi à la romaine* (p. 71) it is best with butter.

BOUILLADE OR ALL GRENAT

This is the Catalan sauce in which snails are cooked in the Roussillon district, and also fish, making a kind of *Bouillabaisse*.

In a tablespoon of olive oil and one of pork fat, sauté 2 or 3 chopped sweet red peppers; when they are soft add 4 or 5 cloves of garlic crushed with the point of a knife, and simmer 2 or 3 minutes. Pour over a small glass of white wine and let it reduce for 1 or 2 minutes; stir in a tablespoon of flour to bind the sauce

* The best substitute for meat glaze or meat stock. It can be bought at large stores.

and cook gently for 10 minutes, adding a little water if the sauce gets too thick.

BEURRE DE GASCOGNE

In a small pan of salted water boil about 6 cloves of garlic. Let them cook for 15 minutes, then strain them, pound them in a mortar and add 1 oz or so of good dripping. In Gascony, of course, they use pork lard, but any good meat dripping will do. When the garlic and the dripping are well amalgamated, add a tablespoon of chopped parsley.

This sauce is stirred into cooked haricot beans, lentils, stewed mushrooms, aubergines, or can be added to soups before serving.

L'AILLADE TOULOUSAINE

Pound 3 oz of skinned walnuts in a mortar with 2 or 3 cloves of garlic; season them with a little salt. Add drop by drop at first, and then more quickly, about 1 gill (5 oz) of olive oil, stirring until you have a thick sauce.

To be served as an hors-d'œuvre with fresh bread and raw celery to dip in the *aillade*, or as a sauce with any cold meat. Goes particularly well with tongue.

PRESERVES

RED-CURRANT AND CHERRY JAM

Put 4 lb of red-currants into a pan without any water and stir them over a gentle flame until the juice comes out. Strain through a muslin without pressing the fruit so that the juice is clear. There should be about 2 lb of juice.

For this amount stone 4 lb of cherries, and make a syrup with 6 lb of sugar and 3 glasses of water; put the cherries into the syrup and let it boil gently until the syrup sets, when put on to a cold plate. Now add the red-currant juice, let the whole mixture boil again, and the jam is ready to put into pots.

These jams made of mixed fruits are very much liked in France, and are often served, with fresh cream, as a dessert.

WATER MELON AND ORANGE JAM

Remove the seeds from a water melon and cut the flesh into squares; for 2 lb of fruit add 1½ lb of sugar and leave this in a basin for 2 or 3 hours, then put it all into a pan and cook slowly for about 1 hour.

At the same time prepare enough oranges to give 2 lb when the skin and pips have been removed. Divide the oranges in quarters, and put them, with the thin peel of 2 oranges cut into strips, into a syrup composed of 2 lb of sugar and a tumbler of water; let this boil gently for 1 hour.

When the two jams are nearly cooked, mix them carefully together, and boil for another 6 minutes before putting the jam into pots. A slice or two of lemon can be added to the water melon while it is cooking, and removed afterwards.

LE CONFITURE DE PASTÈQUE DE LA DORDOGNE

Peel the water melon, take out the pips and cut in thin slices. Weigh the pulp, and for 10 lb add 8 lb of sugar. Leave it to marinate in a bowl with 4 sticks of vanilla and 2 lemons cut in thin slices.

After 24 hours put it all into a preserving pan (removing the vanilla), and cook very slowly for 8–10 hours. Before taking the jam off the fire add a claret glass of rum. Let it boil a few minutes before putting it into pots.

COTIGNAC ORLÉANAIS

Peel, core and slice 4 lb of quinces. Put them into a preserving pan with water not quite covering them. Bring them to the boil and cook for 30 minutes. Strain them through a muslin, pressing them so as to extract as much juice as possible.

In the juice cook another 3 lb of quinces, peeled, sliced and cored, and 1 lb of oranges, skinned and quartered, with the pips removed. Simmer for 1 hour, and put the mixture through a sieve, so as to obtain a thick purée; weigh the purée, add an equal quantity of sugar, return to the pan and cook until the mixture begins to come away from the sides.

The *cotignac* can be stored in jars or tins.

Excellent eaten with soft cream cheese.

PRUNES IN CHERRY BRANDY

Into a large glass jar put a quantity of the best French prunes or Carlsbad plums. Pour over them some good cherry brandy. The next day pour in some more, as the plums will have absorbed the brandy; and so on for a day or two.

Finally cork it down for a fortnight or so, then serve at dessert. Refill the jar as the plums are eaten.

CHERRIES IN BRANDY

3 lb morello cherries, 1 bottle brandy, ½ lb sugar.

Prepare the cherries, which must not be too ripe, by cutting the stalks, so that there is a small piece left in each cherry. Put them in wide jars, pour over the brandy and screw down the covers. Leave them for 6 weeks in a warm place (in France they are left in the sun).

At the end of this time strain off the brandy and mix it with a syrup prepared with the sugar and 2 or 3 tablespoons of water. Pour this back over the cherries through a muslin or a filter paper and leave them another fortnight before they are ready to eat.

SPICED PEACHES

These are to serve with ham or with cold turkey. The proportions are 3 lb of ripe peaches, 1 lb of caster sugar, ½ pint of water, 6 oz (just over ¼ pint) of Orléans or other white-wine vinegar, cloves, cinnamon, ginger.

Drop the peaches into boiling water for a few minutes, drain them, and peel off the skin, which comes off very easily if the peaches are ripe. Stick a clove into each peach.

Make a syrup of the water and sugar and add a half teaspoon each of ground cinnamon and ginger. Put the peaches in and cook for 10 minutes, then leave to cool. After a few hours drain off the syrup, put it back in the pan and add the vinegar, bring to the boil and simmer for 20 minutes, add the peaches again and simmer until they are just tender, by which time the syrup should have thickened. Leave the peaches to stand overnight in the syrup.

Next day pack them into jars, reheat the syrup and pour it over the peaches. They will keep a long time, but once a jar has been opened it is advisable to keep it in the ice-box.

OLIVES

Both black and green olives are best bought loose, whenever possible, and stored, covered with olive oil, in jars. Small olives are usually better than large ones.

INDEX

ELIZABETH DAVID

A BOOK OF MEDITERRANEAN FOOD

'When you read Elizabeth David, you get perfect pitch. There is an understanding and evocation of flavours, colours, scents and places that lights up the page'
Guardian

A Book of Mediterranean Food – published in 1950 – was Elizabeth David's first book and it is based on a collection of recipes she made while living in France, Italy, the Greek islands and Egypt.

She gives us hearty pasta and polenta dishes from Italy; aromatic and tangy salads from Turkey and Greece; and tasty seafood and saffron dishes from Spain.

Whether it is the simplicity of hummus or the delicious blending of flavours found in plates of ratatouille or paella, Elizabeth David's wonderful recipes are imbued with all the delights of the sunny south.

'Not only did she transform the way we cooked but she is a delight to read'
Express on Sunday

'Britain's most inspirational food writer' *Independent*

ELIZABETH DAVID

ITALIAN FOOD

'No one has ever written so knowledgeably, so inspiringly, or so enthusiastically about food' Clarissa Dickson Wright

Italian Food was an inspiration to British cooks when it was first published in 1954 – and it remains so to this day. Embracing the variety, richness and vibrancy of Italian cooking, with particular reference to regional variations, Elizabeth David provides a magnificent and inspiring collection of favourite dishes as well as those more rarely encountered.

With straightforward recipes for meals such as Piedmontese cheese fondue, fettuccine with fresh tomato sauce and chicken breasts with ham and cheese, this is the authentic taste of Italian food.

'Elizabeth David's clear and unpretentious directions for the enjoyment of good food have never been surpassed' *Daily Mail*

'So beautifully written. Elizabeth David was the first to let us know about the real country cooking of Italy' *Mail on Sunday*

'Above all, Elizabeth David's books make you want to cook' Terence Conran, *Observer*

ELIZABETH DAVID

SUMMER COOKING

'David's books are stunningly well written . . . full of history and anecdote' *Observer*

Summer Cooking – first published in 1955 – is a wonderful selection of dishes for table, buffet and picnic that are light, easy to prepare and based on seasonal ingredients.

Elizabeth David shows how an imaginative use of herbs can enhance even the simplest meals, whether egg, fish or meat, while her recipes range from a simple *salade niçoise* to strawberry soufflé. Finally, chapters on *hors d'œuvres*, summer soups, vegetables, sauces and sweets are full of ideas for fresh, cool food all summer long.

'Britain's most inspirational food writer who ranks among the world's gastronomic greats . . . Elizabeth David's writing shows no sign of losing its potent appeal, attracting as much respect now as when it was first published' *Independent*

ELIZABETH DAVID

FRENCH PROVINCIAL COOKING

'Brilliant reading, enthralling and exciting, as well as great cookery. The ultimate book in every way' Gary Rhodes, *The Times*

French Provincial Cooking – first published in 1960 – is the classic work on French regional cuisine. Providing simple recipes like omelettes, soufflés, soups and salads, it also offers more complex fare such as pâtés, cassoulets, roasts and puddings.

Readable, inspiring and entertainingly informative, *French Provincial Cooking* is the perfect place to go for anyone wanting to bring a little France into their home.

'Readers are plunged, through the passion and skill of her writing, deep into the sights and scents of the markets and kitchens of rural France' *Daily Telegraph*

'A joy to read. David's descriptions of France are so wonderful you can almost smell the garlic' Jilly Cooper, *Sunday Express*

ELIZABETH DAVID

AT ELIZABETH DAVID'S TABLE

The best of the best, from the woman who changed the face of British cooking.

Legendary cook Elizabeth David is the woman who changed the face of British cooking. She introduced a dreary post-war Britain to the sun-drenched culinary delights of the Mediterranean; to foods like olive oil and pasta, artichokes and fresh herbs – foods that have become the staples of our diets today. Her recipes brought colour and life into kitchens everywhere, yet her books never contained any photographs. Now, published for the first time, is this beautiful new collection of her most inspiring, everyday recipes with full-colour photography throughout.

Published to celebrate the sixtieth anniversary of Elizabeth's first book, *At Elizabeth David's Table* has twelve chapters guiding the reader from tasty soups and starters, through to meat, fish and desserts. Sections on successful bread-making, as well as more extravagant dishes, ensure that this will become the cookery bible that you will turn to, time and time again. Interspersed throughout the book are some of Elizabeth's short essays – from how to cook 'fast and fresh' using store-cupboard ingredients, to evocative portraits of French and Italian markets.

He just wanted a decent book to read ...

Not too much to ask, is it? It was in 1935 when Allen Lane, Managing Director of Bodley Head Publishers, stood on a platform at Exeter railway station looking for something good to read on his journey back to London. His choice was limited to popular magazines and poor-quality paperbacks – the same choice faced every day by the vast majority of readers, few of whom could afford hardbacks. Lane's disappointment and subsequent anger at the range of books generally available led him to found a company – and change the world.

'We believed in the existence in this country of a vast reading public for intelligent books at a low price, and staked everything on it'
Sir Allen Lane, 1902–1970, founder of Penguin Books

The quality paperback had arrived – and not just in bookshops. Lane was adamant that his Penguins should appear in chain stores and tobacconists, and should cost no more than a packet of cigarettes.

Reading habits (and cigarette prices) have changed since 1935, but Penguin still believes in publishing the best books for everybody to enjoy. We still believe that good design costs no more than bad design, and we still believe that quality books published passionately and responsibly make the world a better place.

So wherever you see the little bird – whether it's on a piece of prize-winning literary fiction or a celebrity autobiography, political tour de force or historical masterpiece, a serial-killer thriller, reference book, world classic or a piece of pure escapism – you can bet that it represents the very best that the genre has to offer.

Whatever you like to read – trust Penguin.